THE HOMES
OF AMERICA

as they have expressed
the lives of our people
for three centuries

ERNEST PICKERING

New York
THOMAS Y. CROWELL COMPANY

Many of the photographs reproduced herewith were borrowed from several sources and combined with those taken by the author. The majority of the photographs were made available by the efforts of the architects and photographers who worked on the Historic American Buildings Survey and who compiled a splendid documentary record of significant buildings in all parts of the country. The author is grateful for the discerning judgment of these men and also for the assistance of members of the staff of the Division of Fine Arts of the Library of Congress in the selection of the photographs.

The author also wishes to acknowledge the help of his wife in the preparation of the manuscript. Her interest in and memory for historical events made her an ideal critic of the manner in which the brief pageant of American life, as a background for domestic architecture, is presented in this book.

CONTENTS

PROLOGUE . . . THE STAGE IS SET   3

PART ONE . . . THE COLONIAL PERIOD

The New England Colonies

Chapter 1   THE EARLY YEARS   31

2   STARK SIMPLICITY   37

3   GEORGIAN PROSPERITY   61

4   HOUSES FROM HANDBOOKS   66

The Middle Atlantic Colonies

5   THE DUTCH, QUAKERS, AND GERMANS   92

6   VARIATIONS OF A THEME   95

The South Atlantic Colonies

7   THE ROUTE TO RICHES   116

8   SOUTH ATLANTIC GEORGIAN   121

The Spanish and the French

9   THE SPANISH CONQUESTS   143

10   THE ADVENTUROUS FRENCH   149

PART TWO . . . THE NEW REPUBLIC

The Post-Colonial Period

Chapter 11   THE NEW ERA   153

12   THE GEORGIAN CLIMAX   155

13   THE INFLUENCES OF ROME   178

The Greek Revival

14   THE CHANGE IN CHARACTER   186

15   YANKEE AND ANTE-BELLUM MANSIONS   198

PART THREE . . THE ERA OF CONFUSION

More Revivals

Chapter 16   ROMANTICISM   215

17   THE GOTHIC REVIVAL   225

18   THE MELTING POT   235

PART FOUR . . . THE PRESENT CENTURY

Tradition and Function

Chapter 19   ECLECTICISM   241

20   THE RECENT DECADES   253

21   RELEASE FROM TRADITION   261

Index   281

BENJAMIN ABBOT HOUSE
Andover, Massachusetts

The cycle is complete—after three ce
reappearing

mplicity of the early American home is
nporary house.

HOUSE IN CALIFORNIA
R. J. Neutra, architect

PROLOGUE
THE STAGE IS SET

HOMES AS DWELLINGS

THE HOME

The home, either as a dwelling, a social unit, or an abiding place of the affections, has a significance that varies with time, place, and people. As a dwelling, home may be old with historical meaning—retaining the charm, beauty, and dignity with which it was originally endowed—or it may be old with blight and dirt, standing in some backwater of stagnation and by-passed by the stream of growth and progress. In age, it may be new in an ugly, garish, and untruthful manner; or it may be new in a way that is simple and beautiful. In location, home may be part of a city, town, village, hamlet, or farm, located in New England, the South, the Middle West, or the Pacific states.

Home may be an apartment on Park Avenue with a doorman in uniform or it may be a walk-up flat on Third Avenue with flower pots balanced precariously on the window sill. Home may be a small cottage on a narrow lot or a manor house set in the midst of rolling acres. It may be in a slum inhabited by the poor or on an estate built by the wealthy. Whatever it is and wherever it may be located, it is the scene of family life and the center for intimate rest and relaxation. The home touches many phases of our lives; it engages a major share of our thoughts, energies, and resources. Its study challenges our imagination; its intelligent use, our understanding.

THE RECORD

Architectural structures form the most permanent and revealing

3

record of a civilization. The temples and cathedrals tell us how man has worshiped; shops and mills, how he has worked; castles and cottages, how he has lived. A nation's prosperity is reflected in the materials used in its buildings; the complexity of its culture appears in the variety of its structures. On the pages of a nation's architectural history are recorded its vehicles of transportation, its occupations and professions, and its religion and education. Here we may read of the soul of a nation, of either its materialism and uninspired construction or its spiritual achievements and its great contributions to the art and science of building.

Hence, buildings are not created in a vacuum. Many and varied influences have shaped the growth of architectural movements. Some of the influences of science, religion, education, or industry upon the development of the homes of this country are direct and obvious; others are more devious and, if they are to be discovered, must be deliberately and carefully traced. Some of these influences we shall discuss; others we shall only suggest.

It is necessary to mention only a few of the influences immediately outside the sphere of family life to discover their importance in the development of domestic architecture. Methods of communication have determined the speed with which new ideas of design and construction spread to distant regions. Improvements in transportation have encouraged the shipment of building materials and have minimized the development of an indigenous architecture. With each succeeding generation the science of illumination and heating has increased the comfort of homes. Wars, depressions, and periods of prosperity have changed standards of living and the attitudes and practices of entire nations. New processes and instruments have been tested in war and successfully adapted for peacetime use. The housewife of today benefits by the experiments of industry and government for offense and defense. Family life and family shelter cannot escape the influences of new types of recreation, occupations, and education. Thus the home develops as an integral part of a social environment.

In a similar manner, our domestic architecture is one of the elements of a physical environment and as such must yield to the steady pressure of its many ingredients. Climate, with its heat and cold, drought and rain, wind and sun, teams up with geography, with its oceans, mountains, and plains, to produce a setting in which man builds his home. Surrounded by these tangible and insistent influences, man must use his tools and knowledge to produce a desirable type of shelter. The erection of a house is an attempt to capture the most friendly and pleasant and to minimize the unfriendly and unpleasant qualities of climate and geography. This is the place of the home in a physical environment.

FOR MANY CENTURIES

In addition to its position in a physical and social environment, domestic shelter takes its proper place in the broad stream of architectural development. The architecture of our homes has not sprung full grown from the resourcefulness and creative ability of each generation of builders. Instead, it is part of a steady procession of styles and movements which have had their beginnings in previous ages and to which many variations have been added by man in his search for an expressive architecture.

Thus architecture has developed by progressive growth from the days of antiquity to those of the present, except during the Renaissance when literature, art, and architecture sought inspiration in the dignity and monumentality of the Classical. Then architecture looked backward instead of forward and for several hundred years the designers of public, religious, and domestic buildings of first Europe and then America borrowed freely from the past. Only during recent years has there been a promise of the first really new architectural movement since the Gothic period of the Middle Ages.

The periods of architectural growth may be classified according to the structural systems used. The Egyptian and Greek styles employed the post and lintel or the columnar and trabeated type (vertical support and horizontal beam) as the basis for construction. The structure was straightforward in its expression and had not yet reached the complexity of treatment which was to follow in later periods. Greek architecture, which was to influence the design of American homes in the nineteenth century, thus achieved a unity of purpose and simplicity of composition reflecting the Greek ideal of beauty in all forms of creative endeavor.

Later the Romans developed their version of the Classical by retaining the column and entablature (beam or horizontal band of moldings) of the Greeks and adding the arch, vault, and dome. These new elements gave more freedom to planning and enabled Roman builders to span greater distances with their architectural forms.

Following the decline of the Roman Empire, the Romanesque style developed in western Europe. This style was symbolized by the round arch and vault; but its builders, in laying up the courses of dressed stone, used the principle of equilibrium instead of the one of inert stability. In other words, a system in which stone is held in place by a balanced arrangement was substituted for that which used only the primitive principle of simply putting one piece of stone on top of another.

The Gothic style of medieval architecture evolved from the Romanesque and was distinguished by the pointed arch and supporting buttress. This style was the culmination of the movement away from massive stability, which began with the temples, toward lightness and flexibility, which ended with the soaring, equipoised vaults of the cathedrals.

Later the Renaissance movement was a rebirth of the Classical theme, a movement which used the familiar forms of the Romans but played them in a different key. Here was the definite break in the continuous evolution of architecture in Europe which had begun with the buildings of antiquity and had persisted for at least two thousand years. While the columns, pilasters, entablatures, balustrades, and arcades of Roman architecture were not copied slavishly, and while many interesting and novel compositions were secured in the palaces and churches of the period, nevertheless the Renaissance style was a derivative one in structure and appearance. However, each country gave to it a distinct flavor which accounts for the difference between the Renaissance buildings of Italy, France, and England. In the latter country, the movement found expression in the styles which we have called Elizabethan, Jacobean, Classic, and Georgian. The houses built during the Georgian period in England were to be the inspiration for many of the eighteenth-century homes in this country.

After the Renaissance movement and its aftermath there came a century of confusion which witnessed revivals of the Classical, Gothic, and Romanesque styles and their artificial adaptation for the public buildings and homes of the period. And now in the twentieth century there is evidence that the present movement of nontraditional or nonderivative architecture is looking to the future and not to the past, and it seems as if the evolution of architectural forms, interrupted by the Renaissance, is about to be resumed.

In America we can trace the history of three hundred years of architectural development in the houses of each generation of builders. The architecture of the seventeenth century was tentative and experimental, but during the eighteenth century the various expressions of the Colonial style came into full bloom. The first half of the nineteenth century saw the climax of the Georgian and the brief flowering of the Classical forms of the Greek and Roman styles. Then followed the decades of Victorian thought and action, with domestic architecture reflecting the decadent public taste of the period. Finally, the present century has brought Eclecticism and the contemporary movement.

PEOPLE

A history of American homes is necessarily a history of American life. It is not possible to write understandingly of the houses of this country without a knowledge of the people who lived during the important periods of architectural development. Therefore, in order to appreciate the significance of domestic architecture, we shall establish a setting for our homes against a backdrop of the lives of those who followed our geographical and economic frontiers. We shall write about people as they came from the smallness of Europe into the vastness of America to find a continent full of the riches of nature. These were not the riches of the Orient, already developed by a civilization centuries old when America was discovered. Instead they were the forest which awaited the carpenter's ax, the water which was to feel the interruption of the wheel, the fertile prairie which was to yield to the plow, and the mineral deposit which was soon to be uncovered by eager miners. We shall write of those who lived through the centuries of growth and who built homes across the face of the land.

Thus we study the homes of America in a historical and chronological sequence in order to learn about the different architectural treatments and about the people who produced them. We study the homes of yesterday and today for the purpose of establishing a

basis for judging the newer movements which will create the homes
of tomorrow. We shall leave to others any final decision in the con-
troversy between the traditionalist and the modernist, remembering
only that there is little defense for the extreme protagonist of any
movement. The traditionalist is fanning the embers of a dead fire but
the modernist who scorns the experiences of the past ignores much
of the meaning of life and of architecture. Those travelers who look
only straight ahead do not see the beauty and significance of the
things along the side of the road. It is well to pause at the top of the
hill and look back at the valley below. Here much of the fine
architecture of the world will be found; here is enjoyment which
might be missed by those impatient for the new experiences of the
future.

SPACE

Before the coming of the pioneers, much of America was unpene-
trated by human activities. It was natural space in which the cycles
of animal and vegetable life were uninterrupted by the instruments
and practices of a civilization. Into this unspoiled natural space there
came late in the sixteenth and early in the seventeenth century the
early major penetrations by white people. These penetrations were
at first exploratory and curious; later they became insistent and determined. They followed the coast line and the inland waterways,
at least until the Indian trails were comparatively safe for travel. On
the coast and along these trails, clearings were made for simple—and
frequently temporary—shelter and for adjoining fields. This was the
beginning of the conquest of the land. Usually the conquest had a
precarious start, with the fate of the settlement often depending upon
the friendliness of the Indians, the outcome of a crop, the luck of a
hunting expedition, or a shipment of tools and skilled artisans from
across the seas. It was largely a two-dimensional penetration, with
the dwellings generally of an unimportant nature.

It was inevitable, and desirable, that penetrated space should soon
develop into organized space. An advanced type of social order does
not usually grow from the primitiveness of a two-dimensional penetration. Civilization demands the protection and encouragement of
complete shelter characteristic of organized communities. The rude
huts of the early settlers soon gave way to more comfortable houses

Fig. P-1. An early Swedish log cabin near Darby, Pennsylvania. Mid seventeenth century. This familiar and romantic type of house became the home of the frontiersman as he penetrated new and undeveloped country during the conquest of America.

Fig. P-2. A later and more permanent type of house built as the country became settled. The Captain Samuel Taylor house, near Harrodsburg, Kentucky.

(Fig. P-2) and these grew in number until villages came into being. The trails became roads and, in turn, the roads became streets as buildings of various types multiplied in number. Everywhere there was evidence of the hand of man altering the face of nature.

WAVES OF MOVEMENT

The major movements of people which penetrated America varied in time and location with incentives and opportunities. These movements may be divided roughly into two waves, the first belonging to the seventeenth and eighteenth centuries, the second occurring in the nineteenth century. The first was largely agricultural in character, the second was industrial. The first was toward the West, the second combined westward movement with the consolidation of the gains already secured.

Even before the English were colonizing the eastern seaboard, the armies of Spain were penetrating the Gulf and Pacific coasts; and French explorers, traders, missionaries, and soldiers were establishing outposts along the St. Lawrence, the Great Lakes, and the Mississippi (Fig. P-3). These two nations spread their resources too thin and the vast empires that they tried to establish did not survive for long.

Instead, the most significant phase of the first wave of penetration occurred along the eastern seaboard during the seventeenth century when the Stuart kings sent colonists in numbers sufficient to secure a firm foothold in the New World and to insure the establishment of permanent settlements. In Massachusetts these English settlers cleared the land and built the simple homes which we now call Early American (Fig. P-5). Later they looked beyond their own rocky coast to the more fertile valleys (Fig. P-6) and, finding trails and waterways, ventured inland to construct other communities.

To the south, the colonies of Maryland, Virginia, Georgia, and the Carolinas were founded by other English adventurers who established a landed aristocracy with magnificent manor houses along the rivers of the Tidewater area and the low country and beautiful town houses in the cities (Fig. P-7). These settlers, in search of a mineral wealth, found instead one of the soil and developed a plantation life based on an economy of slave labor.

At the same time, the Dutch, turning envious eyes upon the New

FIG. P-3. Ambitious French settlers, traders, and missionaries established a vast empire on the shores of the Great Lakes and the Mississippi River. At Ste. Genevieve, Missouri, is the Bolduc house built about 1750 and moved in 1785.

FIG. P-4. The old Treasury house in St. Augustine, Florida, is a reminder of the attempts of the Spanish to establish a colonial empire in the Southeast. Mediterranean type of architecture.

Fig. P-5. The early settlers in New England built simple, sturdy houses, with central chimneys and overhanging second floors, as evidence of their conquest of the rocky shores of Massachusetts. Above is the early seventeenth-century Scotch house at Saugus.

Fig. P-6. As relative peace and security were established, finer and more substantial homes were constructed. Below is the Hezekiah Chaffee house, Windsor, Connecticut.

FIG. P-7. The early South Atlantic settlements led to the establishment of magnificent estates and town houses, such as the Pelzer house, Charleston, South Carolina.

FIG. P-8. The sturdy Dutch burghers built low, rectangular dwellings with stone walls and dormer windows. The simplicity of the architecture was in keeping with the lives of these early settlers from Holland. Bruin house, Kerhonkson, New York. Mid eighteenth-century building.

World, established themselves at the mouth of the Hudson River and spread northward to the Mohawk (Fig. P-8). In the latter area they built settlements, traded with the Indians, and shipped grain from manorial estates to New Amsterdam and thence to foreign ports.

These activities of the Spanish, French, English, and Dutch complete, except for minor omissions, the early conquest of southwestern and eastern America. They resulted in the establishment of two frontiers, one on the Atlantic coast populated largely by the English, the other in the Southwest sponsored by the Spanish. English culture was to survive and grow, the others were to be absorbed by the first as generations of American life passed and as American history unfolded.

If the seventeenth century was one of tentative footholds ar penetrations along the coast lines, the eighteenth century was one exploration and consolidation. In addition to the increased immigration of settlers from Europe to swell the population of the towns and villages along the Atlantic seaboard, a conspicuous phase of eighteenth-century growth was the movement of people who tu from their established homes to regions beyond the last settlem The conquest of new frontiers by the pioneers, by their children, anu by their children's children gave a vitality to American life which made possible the founding of agricultural and industrial empires and the building of magnificent houses. The architecture of the early homes came under the influence of this vigor and, in spite of the copying and borrowing of European styles, American domestic architecture grew along distinctive national lines.

In time, thought, and action the eastern colonies belonged to the eighteenth century. In the same sense, the nineteenth century can lay claim to the western territories and states. The second wave of immigration and migration came in the nineteenth century and consisted of two distinct parts. One was the influx of immigrants from many parts of Europe who were attracted by the opportunities accompanying the Industrial Revolution of the nineteenth century. The other was the movement of the English, Dutch, Germans, and Scotch-Irish, who pushed beyond the old frontiers of the eighteenth century toward the challenges of the West.

Western America prepared for decades of boisterous and virile development—a development without the comparatively serene and

P-9. Peter King cabin, Chewelah, Washington, from an old print. Built in the nineteenth century during the early days of the taming of the Pacific Northwest. The man and the rifle in the foreground suggest the primitive nature of the region and the dangers encountered in crossing the plains and mountains.

deliberate growth of colonial America which produced the dignity and gracefulness of New England architecture. The homes of the West were often as nondescript in their design as were the raw frontier towns of which they were a part.

During the last half of the nineteenth century the tide turned. People and goods began to move eastward. The plains and the Rocky Mountains had been crossed; the Pacific Ocean had been reached (Fig. P-9). The return journey was made comparatively easy by the building of the railroads. The resources of natural wealth were tapped by the ingenuity of the American people; industry, trade, and business took their places alongside those activities associated with fertile fields and abundant fish, fur, and timber. Those returning from the West met the unskilled workers coming from Europe; the melting pot produced a new generation of Americans and brought social changes which were reflected in the homes of the period.

THE SETTLED AREAS

As the result of repeated penetrations and the growth of established communities, the population of the colonies and later of the states grew at an ever accelerating rate; the settled areas spread westward from the Atlantic coast. At the beginning of the eighteenth century the settlements, which contained the homes of America, were confined in New England to the regions along the coast and up the Merrimac and its tributaries. In New York, communities were established up the Hudson to Albany; while in the South Atlantic area the settlements covered the Tidewater region to the "fall line" of the rivers. The location of the homes of America at this time is shown in Fig. P-10. The population of the country at this time was approximately one-quarter of a million people. By the middle of the eighteenth century, settlers had pushed into central Pennsylvania, the Carolinas, and the Piedmont region. The population had now reached a figure of about a million and a quarter.

At the beginning of the nineteenth century the line of settlements extended from the coast of Maine westward to include most of Vermont, New Hampshire, New York, and Pennsylvania, and along the Ohio River to central Kentucky, and then southeast through eastern Tennessee to the coast of Georgia. The population of the United States at that time was approximately four million people.

By 1800, America was a land of all types of settlements—a land of frontiers, farms, villages, towns, and cities. The large cities gave the new republic a dignity, a sense of fitness, and a feeling for leadership which augured well for the future of the western world. Here were built the magnificent homes of the leaders in trade, industry, and politics.

By 1850 the population of the country had increased to over twenty-three million and the settled area covered most of the territory east of the Mississippi River, as shown in Fig. P-10, and extended westward into the eastern edge of Texas, Kansas, and Nebraska.

During the one hundred years from 1850 to 1950, the population of the United States increased more than sixfold; and, for these many millions of people, homes of all types have been built in all parts of the country. On the plains and in the hills and mountains, on the seacoasts and along the inland streams are the dwellings of the rich and poor; no habitable area has escaped the attention of the American home builder.

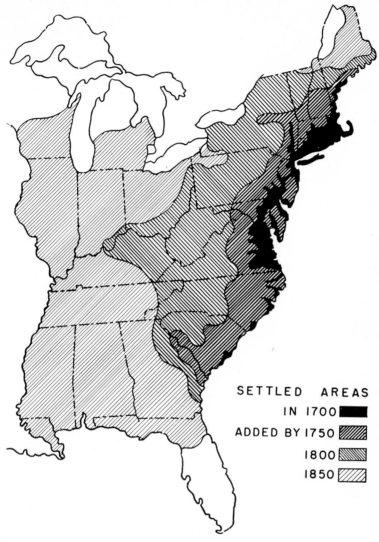

Fig. P-10. The settled areas east of the Mississippi River in which the homes of America were built during the first two hundred years of the existence of this country.

HOMES AND GEOGRAPHY

LOCATION

THE backdrop against which may be seen the homes of America has as a major part of its design the influences of geography—the physical aspects of the country with its resources and climate related to its people and their activities. An important factor in the development of a community of homes is that of location, which determines a town's command of natural resources and other geographical or topographical features adjacent to it. Thus the chief activity of a community may be identified with industry, recreation, mining, shipping, or business—from this activity grows the general character of the town or city and, to some extent, of its homes. As the result of location, together with other factors, New Bedford with its harbor became the home of whaling vessels; Duluth grew because of the adjacent iron ore and water route to eastern furnaces; and Kansas City developed into a packing center because of its proximity to the grazing lands of the prairies. New Orleans, with its good harbor at the terminus of the Mississippi River traffic, has become a seaport for South American trade; while Miami Beach with its climate and beaches has grown into a resort city of hotels and villas.

The manifestations of climate—rain, wind, heat, cold—may encourage or discourage the growth of a region. They may influence the occupations of people, the quality of their life, and the character of their communities and homes. Those people living in the zones of extreme climates—in the frigid north or the tropical south—have little time or energy for the fulfillment of those needs beyond the bare necessities of life. Theirs is a constant struggle against the forces of nature, against the cold of the tundra, the heat of the desert, or the humidity of the swamp—a struggle which is not conducive to the development of an advanced type of domestic architecture. Fortunately most sections of America are temperate in climate and, within the home, the alternating seasons of heat and cold are kept under control.

The early homes of America reflected life as it was lived in the cool woods of New England and the steaming bayous of the Deep South or on the hot prairies of the Mississippi Valley and the foggy shores of the Pacific Northwest. Climate and geography combined to retard the development of communities of homes in the Tidewater area of Virginia. Here was a mild climate for the growing of a single staple crop, tobacco. Here were the rivers and bays into which the ships from England could sail directly to the docks of the individual plantations. The planters did not need the commercial town for the transaction of business. Instead their dealings were directly with London which was closer in interest, if not in distance, than some nearer community isolated by the absence of roads.

As a result, the influences of life in the average community were missing in the affairs of the Virginia colony. Absent were the simple things which characterized the New England village—the town gossip, the meeting in the public tavern, and, more important, the middle class of merchants, skilled artisans, and professional people. Thus the South Atlantic colonies remained, for a long time, a land of extremes—of ruling aristocrats and subservient slaves. There was little of the leavening influence of the middle class. The houses were manorial in their magnificence; the modest houses typical of New England did not appear in Virginia until the pressure of changing economic conditions brought about the development of towns and cities. Climate and geography held out against external influences for several generations.

CLIMATE AND HOUSES

During the first few winters that the Pilgrims spent in New England, there was little progress made in the construction of adequate shelter; but as the vagrancies of the weather were anticipated and understood, a more presentable form of domestic architecture began to emerge from the limited knowledge of materials and construction. And likewise through the succeeding generations—from the beginning of historical development three hundred years ago to the present century—the designs of American dwellings have been adjusted to both the friendly and unfriendly effects of climate. Climate has influenced the plan arrangement of the house, the materials of its walls, the methods of its construction, and the character of its exterior treatment. This was especially true of the homes of earlier years; the influences of climate are less pronounced in the homes of today. Science has pointed the way to a solution of the difficulties imposed by unfriendly nature upon house construction and design. Modern building methods have made it possible to ignore, to a large extent, the snow loads on roofs and the excessive rainfall against walls. Insulation has rendered thick walls unnecessary as a barrier against cold and heat, while air conditioning continues the campaign to secure comfort even beyond that afforded by other means.

Thus through all the periods of American history, climate has, in varying degrees, affected the habits of people and the character of their dwellings. In general, a mild climate produces outdoor living and an architecture that is open in character and rambling in plan. Extreme heat or cold may drive people under shelter and force the enclosing or covering of circulatory elements. In Virginia, however, the weather offered no objection to the removal of the kitchen from the house itself and its placement in a separate building some distance from the main unit, as in the Wythe house, Williamsburg, Figs. P-11 and P-12. This arrangement isolated the noise, confusion, and odors of cooking which might offend the senses of the aristocratic planter and his guests. Encouragement was given to this arrangement by ample slave labor which provided the attendants to carry the steaming tureens and covered platters from the cookhouse to the dining room. Other services were located in separate and flanking structures, as at Shirley (Fig. P-13), Mount Airy (Fig. 8-6), and Stratford Hall (Fig. 8-11). Thus climatic and economic conditions combined to influence the design of eighteenth-century homes in Virginia.

In the early nineteenth-century homes of the Deep South, shown in Figs. 15-8 through 15-16, we find other examples of architecture bowing to the will of climate. The deep porticoes, which often completely surrounded the house, shaded the various rooms from the hot

FIG. P-11. The George Wythe house was the home of Jefferson's law tutor. It was a typical town house of the Revolutionary period and stands today as it did when Washington and Lafayette planned the Yorktown campaign there. House and dependencies from the garden.

FIG. P-12. An example of how a mild climate encouraged the separation of the services from the house itself. Here are the kitchen, smokehouse, laundry, and shops of the Wythe house, Williamsburg, Virginia.

sun and provided places for quiet seclusion on a summer afternoon. The wide central hall, which usually ran entirely through the house from front to back, encouraged circulation of air, a movement which was assisted by the large windows in the rooms on the first floor. In both the Tidewater region and the Gulf states, the spaciousness of the mansions, so desirable for entertaining, was made possible by the mildness of the climate. It was not necessary to conserve heat, as in the North; and, as a result, there were no restrictions against open plans and high ceilings.

The contemporary type of one-story house in California is a direct attempt to capture the pleasant qualities of that famous climate. A house in this indigenous style is likely to have an entire side of the living area open to the outdoors, as in Fig. P-14, facing, perhaps, toward a distant view of mountains or ocean. There is little attempt to separate indoor from outdoor living. As a result, living habits are often reduced to a fundamental simplicity in keeping with an existence close to the elements of nature outside. It is only when this style house is transplanted to a more rigorous climate that incongruity and discomfort may be encountered. It is then that care must be taken to secure proper adjustment between the architecture of man and the forces of nature.

If we turn now to the North, we find that climate was instrumental in developing a type of architecture different from that in the South. The severe winters in New England caused a contraction rather than an expansion of the plan elements of the house itself. Houses were compact rather than rambling in arrangement, as in Fig. P-16. Slaves were not plentiful enough to form the procession from the cookhouse to the dining room, and even if they had been, the rigorous winters would have discouraged such a practice. The kitchen was, consequently, placed close to the dining room for convenience and also as a concession to the weather—a practice which prevails in most of the homes of this country today regardless of the climate. In the homes of the early settlers, the kitchen was the center of home life because here was the warmth of the fireplace in front of which the daily chores were performed and conversation was fostered. In this room and also in others, the ceilings were low and the areas of the rooms small in order to conserve the heat from the central chimney and fireplace.

Fig. P-13. Shirley, Charles City County, Virginia. Early eighteenth-century Georgian mansion with detached dependencies, such as kitchen, laundry, and storage, made possible by a mild climate.

Fig. P-14. House in Santa Barbara, California. Richard J. Neutra, architect. Skillful interpenetration of man-made architectural space with that of nature, encouraged by a friendly climate. (*Photo by Julius Shulman.*)

Fig. P-15. Farmhouse and dependencies, Red Beach, Maine. The house, service wing, and barn are all connected as one unit. This is an example of the influence of severe winters on the planning and design of homes. Early nineteenth-century house, showing Cape Cod derivation.

Fig. P-16. Knight-Short house, Newbury, Massachusetts. A compact type built in 1717 as an expression of the frugality of the Puritan stock and the climate of New England.

Many of the homes of nineteenth-century New England—with some of those of the present responding to the same influence—were built as self-sufficient units for farm life, somewhat reminiscent of the farm buildings of Normandy except for the architectural treatment. Because of the severe winters, the house, milk room, woodshed, and barn were connected as a single structure of varying masses and shapes, as in Fig. P-15. The activities related to the care of man and beast were thus carried on under one roof and it was possible to perform all the chores without the competition of winter winds and snow.

In many of the architectural styles of the past, it is possible to trace the influences of climate upon the choice of materials and structural system. The thick adobe walls and small windows of the houses in New Mexico provided insulation against the heat of the desert. The projecting cornices of buildings of Renaissance origin served as a decorative accent and also as protection for the walls below. In the early homes of New England, the windows were kept small because of the scarcity of glass and also because of the heat loss during the severe winters. In the regions of heavy rain and snow fall, the roofs were likely to be steep to provide a strong structure and a good surface for shedding the moisture. In the countries with a warm climate and brilliant sunshine, the roofs were often less steep and were composed of colorful tiles selected for their decorative effects.

CUSTOMS AND TRADITIONS

As those who settled America moved from one place to another, they built communities which varied greatly in size, character, and importance. In New England there were the colonial villages with their white houses and stately elms surrounding the green. There were also the mill towns, the seaports, and the fishing communities. In the Middle West were the frontier towns with their dusty Main Streets lined with false fronts and their frame houses straggling out into the prairie. Today our citizens live in many types of communities—in rural hamlets, villages, and towns, and in large cities which form the nuclei of even larger metropolitan regions.

Communities, together with their homes, have achieved their present character because of the varied influences of the social, as well as the physical, environment which makes up our cultural pattern. In addition to economic conditions, standards of living, occupations, and the many other aspects of our social order, the customs and traditions, which have been an integral part of American life for generations, play an important role in the development of our domestic architecture.

These customs and traditions may be grouped in two general classes—those which have been inherited and those which have grown out of current practices.

Inherited customs are definitely related to racial, religious, and economic groups. For example, the early settlers from the Palatinate —the Pennsylvania Deutsch or Dutch—bequeathed to their descendants traditions of long standing in the matter of plain and fancy cooking. Their "seven sweets and seven sours" made their kitchens romantic and fragrant pages from old cookbooks; while their heavy meals of *Schnitz 'n Knepp, Kartoffel Kloesse,* and *Fastnacht Kucka* were sources of delight to the true gourmet. This love for substantial food pushed the kitchen and pantry into a very important place in the homes of those sturdy farmers in eastern Pennsylvania.

In a similar vein, southern hospitality is more than a figure of speech. It suggests fried chicken, hickory-smoked ham, and beaten biscuits; it is a warm and genuine welcome which has survived since the period of the old plantations. It suggests space in the house for entertaining the many guests attracted by the warm friendship of the families of the Deep South. Also, the frugality of frontier days is still reflected in the canning and preserving of the produce from the garden and orchard carried on in the rural homes of New England and the Middle West. In addition, the foreign born brought to this country many interesting and delightful customs related to dining and entertaining, and their second generation in our large cities have propagated these customs. Thus the activities of family life and, indirectly, the design of domestic shelter are affected by these inherited customs.

The second group of customs and traditions has grown more directly from contemporary practices. These practices and their accompanying implements come from a knowledge of and ability to use the devices of science, invention, education, transportation, communication, and recreation in our daily activities. Every major change or improvement in any field of human endeavor is reflected in other fields. Our recreational habits—and consequently our homes —are affected by the movie, radio, and television. Our work places and our dwellings come under the direct influence of the automobile and airplane and of the sciences which make them possible. New patterns of living—new traditions—are thus established. Old customs are modified as new ideas appear in the fields of illumination, food preparation, condensed education, or any of the other many instruments of a daily existence. The designs of our homes reflect the current social order.

FUNDAMENTAL NEEDS

We who dwell in the modern cities of America are not much different in our needs and desires from the natives who live in the primitive villages of tropical countries. We in America eat, sleep, work, and play, but so do the people of the Fiji Islands. Our family life is centered in a comfortable house while theirs may be in a one-room hut. Nevertheless the daily activities of all are motivated by the same desire for physical and spiritual satisfaction; the Colonial house in Kansas City and the thatched hut in Namosi Village are built as a setting for the various phases of a daily existence. The basic needs or desires which are connected with home life may be classified as those which are physical—for protection, convenience, and comfort—and those which are spiritual, for social intercourse.

Houses are built to provide shelter as protection against unfriendly climate and as a setting for family life. In the United States, shelter is necessary for protection against the physical discomforts which come from the heat of the sun, the force of the wind, the coldness of the snow, and the annoyance of insects. Protection does not end with the construction of a barrier against the unpleasant elements of nature; protection includes provisions to ward off the unfriendly and undesirable attentions of strangers. We feel more secure in a house with the doors and windows locked than we do in a tent. We need the physical barrier to encourage an unmolested family life. Adequate physical protection also permits the development of a feeling of pride in the present and confidence in the future. The ownership of a comfortable house promotes a sense of satisfaction and security, especially when accompanied by an adequate income to provide financial freedom.

Much of the progress in the design of houses has probably been due to the desire of people for greater convenience in performing everyday tasks. Today many factors contribute to the working convenience of a modern home. Some of these are: proper equipment for the activities of each member of the family, kitchen and laundry with adequate labor-saving devices, ample storage space for work utensils for the housewife, convenient storage for garden tools, and work and storage space for the things related to personal hobbies. Proper relationship between wall areas and window and door openings permits the convenient placing of furniture for conversation, reading, or games. Good circulation, which minimizes the interference of furniture, contributes to convenience in movement. Today much of American life is based on the desire for improved techniques in living in the home.

Another basic desire, which increases in intensity as standards of living are raised, is for physical comfort beyond that provided by mere convenience. The shell of the house affords comfort as a shelter against the weather but the shell also encourages the development of practices, customs, and equipment which contribute to still greater comfort. Modern facilities for heating and illumination and present-day upholstered furniture would not be possible in a cave or hut.

Comfort is a relative term. It is a quality or a condition which is geared to the mechanics of a culture and to a standard of living. The Georgian house of New England provided comfortable shelter in terms of eighteenth-century ideas and demands. The contemporary house reflects the standards by which we live in the twentieth century. A simple existence produces a simple shelter; a complex social culture calls for a complete shelter. Modern family life has left the practices and equipment of a primitive existence far behind. Today we live more comfortably than did those who cooked over an open fire in a cave or before a fireplace in the kitchen. No longer do we squat on the ground and eat from earthen bowls or sit in a smoky hut on uncomfortable stools. No longer do we sleep on a pallet in the corner of a cave or in a rude bed in the "hall."

Instead, we take for granted that we shall have the majority of those comforts which are characteristic of twentieth-century civilization—comforts which were unheard of a few generations ago. Today the modern bed with an inner-spring or sponge-rubber mattress is considered essential for comfortable living. There was a time when the four-poster bed with taut ropes as a foundation for homemade bedding was the ultimate in sleeping comfort. We now consider large windows for sufficient light and walls tight against the weather as necessary for a comfortable existence. These commonplace requirements were regarded as luxuries by the early pioneers. Comfort is, therefore, a progressive and not a static condition. It undergoes constant change in the home as science and education modify our way of life and our implements for living.

One of the most important influences instrumental in the development of communities and homes is the need for social intercourse and companionship. As the first step in intimate human relationships, man associates himself with a woman in an accepted partnership. Thereafter the basic elements of the family relationship are the same, whether in the frontier cabin or the modern home. The man builds a house and the woman creates a home. They locate the home near those of friends in order that all may visit and exchange the amenities of a normal social existence. This has been so since early man discovered that his pleasure was greater when his food was eaten in front of the fireplace with his friends as companions and when his clothes, furniture, and house were admired by others in the community. Thus it is from the desire for association with others that the development of the home and the community springs most directly.

WORK AND RECUPERATION

The people who penetrated primitive America and those who built modern America have been concerned with just two types of activity. Yesterday, today, or tomorrow people either work or recuperate; there are no other kinds of activity. "Work" needs no definition; it is a very understandable part of our vocabulary. Work may be pleasant or disagreeable; it may be physical or mental. It may be in the home, office, shop, or factory.

Most of the work activities in the home are performed by women, especially those activities dealing with the traditional household tasks.

The minor maintenance activities about the house may also fall to the lot of the husband, their performance depending upon his financial ability to hire this work done, upon his physical strength, and upon his general attitude toward manual labor. If he is so inclined, he may cut the grass, trim the hedge, plant the garden, or paint the screens.

"Recuperation" is associated with recovery or restoration. The act may be the recovery of health or the restoration of physical and spiritual energy; it may be the regaining of one's material, mental, or moral equilibrium. In its broadest sense, recuperation is an activity which offers relief from work in the factory, office, or home or on the farm. It may be physical rest in the living room or the bedroom, spiritual regeneration in the church, recovery from an illness in the hospital, or relaxation in the theater. Recuperation is carried on during the excess of time and with the excess of energy above that necessary for the activities required for a mere physical existence. It supplements and enhances our daily lives and makes possible a type of civilization above that identified merely with the biological processes.

While the work activities in the home may belong almost entirely to the housewife, the recuperative activities are engaged in by all members of the family. The home is the scene of physical and mental rest for father, mother, and the children. Recuperation or relaxation in the home may be the personal or individual type. This does not require the cooperation of others and consists of such activities as sleeping, reading, or listening to music. Or it may be the social or group-participation type, such as conversation, games, or entertainment. Provision must be made for both kinds of recuperation in the home.

In the dwellings of Colonial, Greek, or Victorian ancestry, or in those of the contemporary movement, Americans have worked, played, and rested; only the methods of performing these tasks have varied with the different periods—varied in response to current techniques and practices.

Part ONE

THE COLONIAL PERIOD
THE NEW ENGLAND COLONIES

Chapter 1

THE EARLY YEARS

THOSE DETERMINED PEOPLE

THE homes of America were built for people whose needs were influenced by climate and conditioned by the techniques and tools of a social order. It is necessary, therefore, to understand the nature of the people of each period and area if we are to realize the significance of the various styles of domestic architecture. We shall begin with those people who came, early in the seventeenth century, to the shores of New England.

For these early settlers this was an important adventure into the wilderness of a new country, an adventure by those who had personal reasons for leaving England to begin another life beyond the seas. There were those who could not tolerate the worldliness of the court of Charles I in secular affairs or the formality of the Church of England in religious matters. A group of these dissenters, known as Separatists, wishing to worship in their own simple way, broke with the church and developed their own interpretation of religious ritual. These were the Pilgrims who came to this country on the historic *Mayflower* in 1620. Another group had a different approach to their moral and religious problems. They believed that changes could be made within the established pattern of behavior and they hoped to achieve reforms without complete separation. However, it was inevitable that the position of these Puritans would become untenable in England and understandable that they should turn to America for freedom of thought and action.

Thus those who came to the shores of the northeastern part of this country were serious and determined men and women, bent upon establishing homes rather than exploring the wilderness. On one hand, they were full of common sense and enthusiastic about the opportunities in the New World; on the other hand, they were often intolerent and forgetful of the very freedom for which they left England. This religious zeal combined with the English flair for political organization made ideal colonists of these early settlers. In spite of the persecution of some who departed from the accepted religious and social precepts of the different communities, a sound social order soon developed which was to have a profound influence upon later generations of American life.

It is natural that, at first, the life of the Pilgrims who landed at Plymouth should have been crude and difficult. In spite of their knowledge of handicrafts and agricultural pursuits and in spite of their immunity to the debilitating effect of hard labor which they had built up during their stay in Holland, only about half of the original hundred persons aboard the *Mayflower* were alive at the end of the first winter. However, those who were left clung tenaciously to the rocky shores of New England; they built crude shelters, planted corn, and cleared the land. They began to conquer the wilderness of the new country. The earliest homes of the colonists were probably conical huts of branches and turf or huts dug into the hillside and covered with bark roofs. Later these huts were enlarged by the use of ridge poles supported on vertical posts. The first dwellings of timber, which followed as soon as these pioneers could fell the trees, were no doubt constructed of logs or planks stood on end and covered with roofs thatched with dried grass or bulrushes from the adjacent salt marshes.

In none of the early records of life in New England do we find any reference to the use of logs laid horizontally. One reason for the absence of this type of construction is the fact that the people of England were not familiar with this method of building. Naturally the colonists did not know about this type of dwelling before coming to this country and neither did they find it waiting for them when they arrived. There have been many efforts to connect the American log cabin with shelter in the Indian villages. It may be romantic to believe that the early colonists copied the homes of the Indians as they did their methods of farming and their skill on the trail, but there is no proof that the Indian tribes in the northeast built in this manner.

In fact, it is now commonly accepted that the traditional cabin with the logs laid horizontally was brought to this country by the Swedes, Fig. P-1, who settled on the Delaware a few years after the landing of the Pilgrims. As these settlers from Scandinavia traded with the colonists to the north in Massachusetts and with those to the south in Virginia, it is natural that they should have given as a heritage to the pioneers of later generations that modest and honest log house which developed so easily from the forests and which became so symbolic of humble American life. But the ingenuity and resourcefulness of the early colonists doomed the first crude shelter to a short life. The simple, substantial frame house which we now call Early American was soon to appear and the social and economic life of the colonies was encouraged by a more comfortable type of structure.

Before the Plymouth colony was many years old, another and more successful attempt at colonization was taking place to the north of the first settlement. This one was conducted by the Massachusetts Bay Company which sent to this country members of the English middle class composed of artisans, farmers, merchants, professionals, and landed gentry. In general, the Puritans were people with means and offered a sharp contrast to the more humble laborers and farmers of which the Pilgrim settlement was composed. They brought tools, livestock, supplies, and even indentured servants. No doubt they intended to establish in America the same social order as the one which was left behind, substituting for the aristocracy of title one based upon the possession of personal goods. It is possible that the investors in the Massachusetts Bay Company hoped to build large estates, similar to those in Virginia, with gentlemen, tenants, laborers, servants, and slaves. But they overlooked the influences of soil, climate, and building materials upon the economy and architecture of the colony. They found that the stony soil of New England did not permit the raising of a single large staple crop, such as the tobacco of Virginia or the cotton of the South, that the climate permitted only diversified crops, and that the clearing of the land furnished the lumber for the simple frame houses which provided adequate but not grandiose shelter for the modest farmer and merchant. They discovered that their idea of a modified feudal system was impossible in New England and that they must leave to Virginia the privilege of building magnificent manor houses.

The early settlements in the neighboring colonies of Connecticut Rhode Island, and New Hampshire came into existence through the indirect influence of the strenuous struggle for existence in the Massa chusetts Bay area. Dissatisfied with the efforts to wrest a living from the poor soil and irritated by the religious controversies of the period, members of the group migrated to neighboring regions in search of better living conditions. Here they were joined by other Puritans direct from London and thus colonization of New England was on in full force.

COMMUNITY LIFE

Existence in seventeenth-century New England, whether Pilgrim or Puritan, bore considerable resemblance to that in feudal England, except that in America there was no place for the nobility. The early settlers brought with them the social customs with which they were familiar. They did not remain in Europe long enough to see the full effects of the seizure of land by the aristocracy for the purpose of creating baronial holdings. Rather they remembered the use of common land by the peasants for the tilling of the soil; it was this picture of a rural community which they transplanted to the New World. The colonists of each village held a plot of land in common and this was divided into sites for the erection of homes and also into outlying fields for crops. The home sites were large enough for the house, the garden, and perhaps a few fruit trees and berry bushes. These sites were repeated along a single street or road which led to the fields where the men worked during the day. In the center of the dwelling area was usually to be found the church, together with the school located in the parsonage. In an open space near the church was the common pasture, or the commons, which later became the village green of the eighteenth-century colonial village.

It was a communal existence without the presence of the lord of the manor but with the villagers sharing the responsibility for the maintenance of law and order. Thus life in the early settlements was not competitive and there was little difference in the financial and intellectual attainments of the colonists, with the possible exception of the leadership of the minister. Of course, the size of the family and other factors probably dictated the area of the plot assigned for the construction of the home and the size of the house itself. Such matters as topography, prevailing winds, vistas, and deliberate attempts at effective orientation regulated the informal pattern of the village plan. Individual ownership of land was yet to be fully developed; individual initiative and freedom of living were restricted by the strictness of the church and by the spying of those who were always watching for lapses from the established moral code.

The social and intellectual life of the early colonists centered around the church of the village. It was here that these pioneers went for religious worship and for discussions about secular matters. It was in the adjacent parsonage that the youngsters received their meager education. In general, the Pilgrims and the Puritans were a serious people. Their books usually dealt with religious and moral discussions and there was always present an atmosphere redolent with superstitions and supernatural manifestations. There were severe punishments for those who violated the laws of the land—punishments borrowed from the mother country. The stocks and whipping post symbolized the Puritan code of morals and many of the exciting stories of New England life come from the witch hunts of the seventeenth century. With this background, religious ceremonies were particularly austere, since the Puritans had rebelled against the rituals of the Church of England. Music was frowned upon as a worldly and wicked invention and gaiety had little place in the lives of the colonists.

However, in spite of this, the Puritans did not have the extreme religious zeal of the Pilgrims and they did not suffer the same restraint in their attitude toward their dress and homes. While there may have been little to differentiate one group from another, nevertheless it is possible that in the Puritan settlements there was greater freedom in the development of a less barren family life and domestic architecture. In general, however, the clothing of all the early colonists reflected a stern and self-disciplined existence. Since these people turned their backs on the pomp of the English court, naturally they frowned upon the silks, satins, and wigs of the England of Charles I. Brown, gray, purple, and green homespun were the predominant colors in New England and even these were subdued in intensity, giving a traditional drabness to the clothing of the first settlers. The little boys were miniature editions of their fathers and the little girls wore the same kind of simple clothes as did their mothers. It was a period of severe frugality.

Communication between the different settlements was slow and difficult. It was easier to go by water than by the paths which followed the old Indian trails. There were no newspapers and any mail which was lucky enough to get through was carried by travelers. Roads had not yet been built between settlements, and travel by horseback was neither comfortable nor safe. The Puritan and Pilgrim families stayed close at home and family life was simple and self-sufficient. It was, therefore, a period of home industries. During the first decades of life in the American colonies, the specialization with which these people had been familiar in England did not receive the encouragement which was later to come with the development of a reciprocal type of community existence. It was necessary for each family to produce the basic essentials of life—food, clothing, and shelter—together with the furnishings and equipment for an existence above the most primitive. It was necessary for the men to make and use the tools and implements with which the food was secured and processed and for the women to card the wool, draw the flax, and spin the thread. The entire family was a single working unit; all members helping to make the tallow candles, dye the cloth, build the furniture, and prepare the food. The simple homes of seventeenth-century America provided shelter for these basic activities of family life.

Chapter 2

STARK SIMPLICITY

THE huts, hillside homes, and thatched sheds which sheltered the early colonists during the first few years of their life in the New World were soon replaced by houses which, as time and tools made a better type of construction possible, were relatively substantial and comfortable. However, it was not until past the middle of the seventeenth century that the familiar Early American house began to appear in any numbers in the communities of the Pilgrims and Puritans; its influence prevailed until the second quarter of the eighteenth century.

The seventeenth-century house was an example of the direct growth of architecture from function and materials. It was a straightforward solution to the need for simple shelter and was an honest expression of materials. It could be added to as the family increased in size and its interior design permitted its adaptation to the home industries so necessary in a primitive existence. It is logical that the materials used in these houses should be indigenous to the locality and should reflect the abundance of wood as a building material. In general construction and character, these early homes show the influence of the medieval architecture of Europe with which the colonists were familiar (Fig. 2-1); but, as is to be expected, climate and materials combined to produce a dwelling that was fundamentally American. Many of these old houses still stand after nearly three hundred years of existence, houses which are still sturdy in their construction and monumental in their simplicity. To us they may seem stark and bleak but in those earlier days they provided very human and adequate shelter for God-fearing people.

FIG. 2-1. The Pilgrims retained the half-timber construction, steep roofs, overhanging second floors, and small windows with which they were familiar in medieval England Above is a street in Ombersley, Worcestershire.

THE STRUCTURE

While we may not have conclusive records of the character of the temporary homes built early in the seventeenth century, we do not lack information about the homes erected during the last half of the century. In fact, scattered through the states of Massachusetts, Rhode Island, and Connecticut are a number of Early American homes which are well preserved and about which history has given us much pertinent information regarding dates, owners, and early furnishings. The first houses probably consisted of a single room on the first floor with a similar unit repeated on the second floor. The entire structure was built against and as an integral part of a huge chimney and fireplace, as illustrated in the Clemence house shown in Figs. 2-3 and 2-4.

However, most of the houses of the period were larger in size and afforded more space for family activities. The typical plan was a rectangular one and provided for a single room on each side of a central fireplace, with this pattern being repeated on the second floor.

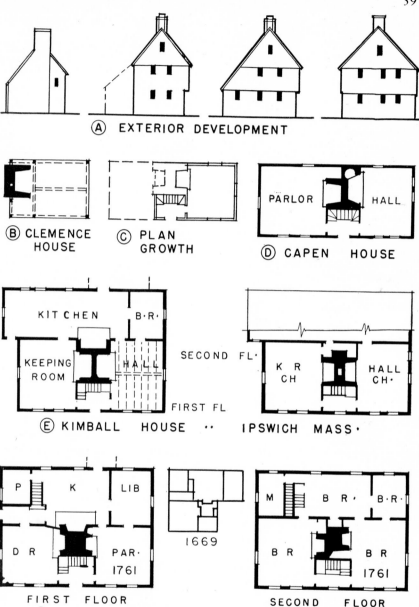

(A) EXTERIOR DEVELOPMENT

(B) CLEMENCE HOUSE

(C) PLAN GROWTH

(D) CAPEN HOUSE

PARLOR   HALL

(E) KIMBALL HOUSE ·· IPSWICH MASS·

KITCHEN   B·R·

KEEPING ROOM   HALL

SECOND FL·

FIRST FL

K R CH   HALL CH·

(F) FISHER-WHITING HOUSE · DEDHAM MASS·

P   K   LIB

D R   PAR·   1761

1669

FIRST FLOOR

M   B R·   B·R·

B R   B R   1761

SECOND FLOOR

FIG. 2-2. Plans of Early American houses, also development of exterior massing. *D* shows early four-room type, while *F* illustrates the completely developed house with rooms at rear.

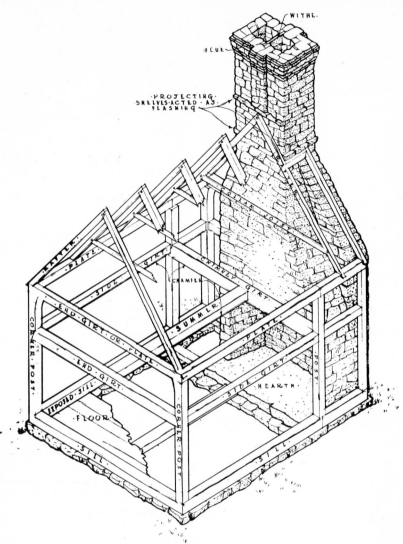

FIG. 2-3. Probable original framing of the Clemence house shown on opposite page. Vertical posts are held together with heavy horizontal beams and the entire structure is built against the stone chimney.

In front of the chimney on the first floor was the entry, or "porch," from which a narrow, winding stairway led to the second floor. Even though the house grew in size and received alterations during suc-

FIG. 2-4. Clemence house, Manton, Rhode Island. Splendid example of 17th century one-unit house. Single room on first floor, with another room in attic space above. Stairway in corner in front of chimney. Note small windows and simple entrance.

FIG. 2-5. Restored window, showing diamond-shaped panes and rough, narrow siding of wall.

FIG. 2-6. Unpretentious wooden door with wrought-iron nails set in a decorative pattern.

Fig. 2-7. Whipple house, Ipswich, Massachusetts. Original one-room house was built about 1640, the remainder before 1682. One of the best-preserved and most typical examples of early homes.

ceeding generations, this was the basic plan and the one that became standardized into a familiar form.

When the family increased in number or when its financial status was improved, an addition was made at the rear of the house in the form of a lean-to, as in Fig. 2-2. The rear slope of the roof of the main part of the house was carried down over the addition and the entire composition was called a "salt box" house. Another fireplace was usually added to the central chimney and the room at the rear became the kitchen. Later houses were often built in their entirety, with the first four rooms and the additional rear unit constructed at the same time, thus providing a larger and more ambitious structure than that typical of the earlier examples. In the John Kimball house at Ipswich, Massachusetts, (Fig. 2-15), is an exterior composition, with the rear roof carrying down to include the rooms at the back of the house.

The large central chimney acted as the core of the structural system and the heavy timbers were framed around it. The chimney and the frame thus helped to support and strengthen each other. In

FIG. 2-8. Early American type house at East Gloucester, Massachusetts. Note central chimney, narrow siding, simple entrance, and decorative pendant drops under cornice.

the early houses the chimneys were built of wood and clay, which accounted for the presence of the inquisitive firewarden who was always peering into the fireplaces looking for fire hazards. Later the chimneys were built of stone and brick, the tops sometimes being terminated with decorative courses of brick reminiscent of the Tudor Gothic. This treatment is shown in Fig. 2-23 in the Parson Capen house at Topsfield, Massachusetts.

The medieval character of these early homes is also reflected in the construction, or framing. The colonists remembered the half-timber houses of England; and, with the abundance of wood, it is not surprising that a solid and substantial framework should be developed similar to that of the Tudor homes of the mother country. The heavy framework was no doubt laid out on the ground by the sturdy craftsmen of the period and then raised in place by the co-operative efforts of neighbors.

The framing consisted of heavy corner posts with connecting horizontal timbers, or beams, pegged together without the use of nails and decorated with chamfering, or the beveling of the corners,

43

FIG. 2-9. Kitchen of the Whipple house, Ipswich, showing the large fireplace which provided warmth and light and a center for work activities of the family. The furniture is typical of the period and harmonizes with the simplicity of the pine paneling and wooden beams.

FIG. 2-10. End view, showing a molded overhang forming an accent at each floor level.

FIG. 2-11. Entrance, with window above. Simple treatment is typical of period.

FIG. 2-12. Detail view of house at East Gloucester. Even though modernized, the quaintness of seventeenth-century days has been retained. See Fig. 2-8.

FIG. 2-13. Fairbanks house, Dedham, Massachusetts. Early house with a complex pla
and irregular massing due to various additions. A portion of the central block wa
built in 1640. The gambrel roof of the left wing, with its two slopes on each side
was a later development.

FIG. 2-14. Morton-Corbett house, Ipswich, Massachusetts. Salt-box type roof. Modifie
overhang on front and at ends. Clustered chimney treatment reveals medieval influenc

Fig. 2-15. John Kimball house, Ipswich. Late 17th-century house with a central chimney and a typical salt-box roof sloping to the rear. The Doric entrance and the size and spacing of the windows reveal a later Colonial influence. Plan in Fig. 2-2.

Fig. 2-16. Fireplace in the "hall" chamber on the second floor, showing the beams, pine paneling with molded edges, and wide flooring boards which were characteristic of the period.

and with bracketing, as shown in Fig. 2-3. The largest beams were called the summer beams and they often had molded corners which gave some relief to the simplicity of the interior treatment. The roof rafters were steep in their pitch, as a concession to the heavy snows of New England and also to the influence of Gothic architecture. One of the most conspicuous characteristics, which disappeared with the coming of the eighteenth century, was the overhang of the second floor. This was another medieval detail and was borrowed from the houses on the narrow streets of English cities, where space was at a premium. The Capen house (Fig. 2-23) shows a projecting second floor in which the lower ends of the second-story corner posts are terminated with decorative drops. In some instances the gable ends were framed to project beyond the lower floors, as in the Whipple house at Ipswich, shown in Fig. 2-10. This detail gave additional variety to the exterior treatment.

The type of filling between the framework, which was to form the protective shell of the building, was again borrowed from medieval England. This filling usually consisted of a wattle composition of interwoven twigs or branches or of wooden laths daubed with clay mixed with straw and finished with a coat of lime plaster to offer the best resistance to the weather. In some instances sun-dried bricks were used for filling. In those Early American houses which are now standing, the half-timber construction with its filling has been covered with wood siding; it is logical to assume that this covering was put in place shortly after the houses were built. No doubt the severe winters of New England soon pointed to the impermanent nature of the plaster-covered walls. In fact, we may question whether any buildings were erected in the true half-timber style with the framing and filling exposed and visible or, if such were the case, that they stood this way for any length of time.

EXTERIORS

Before going inside one of the early homes, let us take a closer look at the exterior. These houses usually stood with the long side, or main elevation, facing the street. Narrow weatherboarding covered the walls, which were pierced at widely separated intervals with small windows arranged somewhat formally around a central entrance. The medieval influence was again reflected in the smallness

FIG. 2-17. Before the simple fireplaces of the first homes in New England gathered the early colonists to perform their many household tasks. Here in the "keeping room" fireplace of the John Kimball house, Fig. 2-15, is embodied the sturdiness of those primitive days.

FIG. 2-18. The dining room fireplace of the Benjamin Lincoln house, Hingham, Massachusetts, represents a hundred years of development and refinement since the days of the Pilgrims.

of the windows, a characteristic encouraged by the scarcity of glass and the severity of New England winters. It is possible that the early houses depended upon shutters or oiled paper for the necessary protection, but by the middle of the seventeenth century casement windows with leaded panes of rectangular or diamond shapes were commonly used.

The moldings of the corner boards and posts and of the cornice were simple in character and the entire exterior had a feeling of austerity and stark simplicity which was in keeping with the lives of the occupants. In the early houses the steep roofs were probably covered with thatch unsuited to a rigorous climate. The abundance of wood no doubt encouraged the early introduction of wood singles as a more permanent form of covering. The typical rectilinear mass of the building was dominated by the central chimney; the cornice line was unbroken except in those examples where several gables were introduced, as in the John Ward house in Salem.

The doorway was usually surrounded by a simple frame and, except for its important location in the composition, was an inconspicuous feature of the exterior, as in Fig. 2-11. The door itself was constructed of two layers of boards, the outer boards being placed vertically while the inner boards were arranged horizontally. Wrought-iron nails were often used to secure a decorative pattern on the exterior, as in the Clemence house shown in Fig. 2-6.

INTERIORS

Let us now enter one of these Early American houses. The low door opens directly into the entry, or "porch." Facing the doorway is the narrow winding stairway which leads to the second floor. On either side of the entry is a rectangular room with a large fireplace. One of these rooms is the "hall," which is the descendant of the great hall of the medieval manor house or castle, while the other is the parlor, which was used chiefly for living and sleeping. The hall was the scene of the major work and recreational activities of the family. The large fireplace, with its timber beam, or lintel, over the opening, furnished the heat, light, and physical cheer for the colonists during

FIG. 2-19 (opposite). Mid eighteenth-century simplicity exhibited in the Samuel Trevett house, at Marblehead, Massachusetts. The same spirit returns in the twentieth-century house by Frank Lloyd Wright, Fig. 2-20.

the long winter evenings. It was equipped with a built-in oven and swinging cranes for the cooking utensils. In it the Pilgrim housewife baked her bread and beans and cooked her venison and corn. Around it gathered the entire family at work—spinning, weaving, repairing, and manufacturing. Around it the necessities of life were processed or made and the family life of the first colonists was nurtured.

The early hearth, with its sturdy and unpretentious design supplemented by its immense size, was the forerunner of the beautiful and graceful masterpieces of the Georgian and Post-Colonial periods. From this first utilitarian fireplace there developed, generation by generation, ever changing interpretations expressing the culture of the times. Here one can read an accurate chronology of the lives of the colonists from Maine to the Carolinas or of the frontiersmen as they moved westward to new opportunities beyond the Alleghenies. Here one can read of the development of an American culture as the simple oak beam over the opening was replaced by the exquisitely carved mantel and the plain pine boards gave way to the beautifully molded panels. Thus, as we turn the subsequent pages to follow the history of America with each generation of home builders, we may trace the material and spiritual progress of our people through the character and treatment of their fireplaces. We may see, as in Figs. 2-17 through 2-20, the completion of a cycle of growth—beginning with the simplicity of the Early American, through the ornateness of the Georgian and the later revivals, and back again to the simplicity of the contemporary movement.

Elsewhere in the Early American house, the interiors of the major rooms were treated as simply as was the fireplace or the exterior design of the structure. Some of the walls were plastered but most of them were sheathed with wide boards, grooved together and molded or chamfered along the edges. These boards were laid either vertically or horizontally, with the vertical direction usually reserved for the partition walls and the horizontal for exterior walls. This treatment, together with the exposed beams, may be seen in the view of the hall chamber of the John Kimball house in Ipswich, shown in Fig. 2-16. In those instances where some of the walls were plastered with a clay daub and finished with a wash of lime, the combination

FIG. 2-20 (*opposite*). Interior of house by Frank Lloyd Wright. The fireplace treatment places the emphasis on essential elements and subordinates applied decoration. (*Photo by Robert Imandt.*)

FIG. 2-21. Stairway, Stephen Daniel house, Salem. Simple treatment typical of period.

FIG. 2-22. Stairway in Kimball house Ipswich. Exterior view is shown in Fig. 2-15.

of white plaster, pine boards tinted to an umber with the smoke and wax of succeeding generations, the color of homespuns, and the gleam of pewter gave to these Early American interiors a quality which would stir the imagination and envy of those who today find romance and beauty in the arts of the past.

The stairways of these seventeenth-century houses repeated the character of the principal rooms. They ascended to the second floor in three short flights, with winders sometimes substituted for landings. The few balusters used were often turned in a simple design and the balustrade usually terminated against a heavy newel post with simple turnings, as in the examples in Figs. 2-21 and 2-22. The turnings of the stairway elements, the molded edges of the boards in the pine paneling, the pattern of nails in the front door, and the carved drops of the overhanging second floor were the only concessions which the strait-laced Puritans made to the cause of ornamentation. Renunciation of the frivolities of Europe and adherence to a frugal existence ruled out the presence of the more decorative aspects of architectural treatment.

The second floor may be dismissed with only a few words of description, since it contained no significant architectural features and since history or present restorations tell us little of special interest about its use and equipment. Usually the first floor plan was repeated on the second level, an arrangement which provided two rooms similar in size and location to the hall and parlor below. Apparently these rooms were used for additional sleeping quarters and for storage purposes.

The low-ceilinged rooms of the seventeenth-century homes of New England contained only the furniture and furnishings essential to basic existence. The early colonists had neither the time nor imagination for anything else. The furniture was of the sturdiest construction and the simplest design. It blended with the rough paneling and received, along with the pine boards of the walls, the patina of time and use. The early furniture had a distinct medieval quality because these Pilgrims and Puritans were not far removed in time, even though in distance, from the influences of the Jacobean, Elizabethan, and William and Mary examples.

The chairs, tables, and chests were often crude and heavy, and had moldings, spindles and legs reminiscent of the Gothic or of the transitional period between the medieval and the Renaissance. Toward the end of the seventeenth century, the Georgian influence was more pronounced and the furniture found in these early homes became more graceful in design and appearance. Those houses which were built early in the eighteenth century, even though they retained the early type of plan with a central chimney, were finished on the interior with paneled wainscots, molded trim, and graceful mantels—details which were the forerunner of the later and more ornate Georgian treatment. In general, the furniture of these later houses followed the pattern established by other interior details, and the sturdy simple chairs and tables were replaced by those of a more sophisticated type.

The furniture of the hall usually consisted of only the essential pieces. Near the fireplace were a few stools, some benches, a table, and the ever present settle whose high back and sides provided protection against the wind which blew through the poorly insulated walls. Nearby was the spinning wheel and the loom. If the room happened to be used for sleeping purposes, there was a bed of either the jack-bed type or the four-poster kind. The jack bed was made

FIG. 2-23. Capen house, Topsfield, Mass. Built in 1683. Plan in Fig. 2-2.

FIG. 2-24. House at Eastport, Maine. Built in 1802. Cape Cod type.

by anchoring a post near one corner of the room at the correct distance from the two adjacent walls and connecting the post to the walls with rails. Slats were added to support a mattress or tick stuffed with rags, feathers, or straw.

The four-poster bed, borrowed from the medieval homes of England, had, as its name indicates, four tall posts at the corners which supported a framework from which was suspended the hangings to enclose the occupants of the bed. These four-posters with their ruffle of gay fabrics around the top are favorites with contemporary interior decorators when Colonial interiors are reproduced for present-day clients. While decoration may be uppermost in the mind of the modern decorator, function was the guiding motive for the housewife of the New England colony. The drapery of the four-poster bed served the very utilitarian purpose of protecting the occupants from the drafts and also provided the privacy which was so scarce in the Early American house. The bed, shown in Fig. 6-8, suggests the functional use just described.

In addition to the furniture previously mentioned, there was the large table near the fireplace which served for eating purposes and for general chores. It usually consisted of several boards or planks supported by legs of the trestle type. On this were to be found a few wooden bowls, pewter tankards, mugs, and plates, and perhaps some spoons and kitchen utensils of iron and pewter.

As important as were the stools, tables, beds, and settle, none occupied a more important place in the life of the family than did the chest. Chests were used for all purposes—for the storage of clothing, tools, and utensils. The early ones were simple, boxlike containers with lids; the later ones were more elaborate and were either imported from abroad or made by local craftsmen. Short legs were added and other refinements were incorporated until the complete chest with turned legs and drawers with ornamental pulls was the accepted and required piece of furniture.

ON CAPE COD

While the familiar two-story houses, commonly called Early American, were being built in southern New England, one small region in this larger area witnessed the construction of an even simpler type which was to become more popular with later builders than the larger version. During the development of the Early American style, simple one-story houses with no projections or overhang were being constructed on Cape Cod. A steep roof with two sloping surfaces, or occasionally one of the gambrel type, covered the rectilinear mass of the building. From this composition projected the customary low, heavy chimney. A central doorway, flanked on either side by two windows, completed the treatment of the main facade. In many cases an unsymmetrical composition was secured by placing the door at one end of the main facade.

A house of this smaller type is shown in Fig. 2-25, from which it is seen that the Cape Cod revival of the present generation bears a striking resemblance to those of this period. The Joseph Atwood house at Chatham, shown in Fig. 2-26, belonging to the transitional period between the Early American and Colonial periods. It was built early in the eighteenth century and its date is betrayed by the more elaborate character of the doorway and by the use of interior trim typical of Georgian architecture. In plan, however, it retains its Early American arrangement.

Just as the familiar Early American house was an expression of local materials and of the needs of the inland Pilgrims, so was the Cape Cod cottage an equally authentic outgrowth of the environment of the windswept Cape. It was a minimum house built by ship's carpenters for the fishermen and shipbuilders who formed the democratic society of this part of Massachusetts. It was such a complete answer to the needs of the early settlers and their descendants that the two-story houses of a more ambitious nature did not appear in this region until after the beginning of the nineteenth century. The Cape Cod house was built of wood because of the absence of stone; and it assumed the low, compact mass in defiance to the driving winds and shifting sands. As stated, it was constructed around the familiar central chimney, which again provided the structural core of the house. In plan, there was usually a large room at the rear which was the kitchen and work area and which also served as the major place of congregation for the family. The other rooms on the first floor, smaller in size, were the parlor and bedrooms, with additional sleeping space provided in the half story under the roof.

FIG. 2-25 (*opposite*). Typical Cape Cod cottage. Its unsymmetrical treatment of doors and windows and single chimney, combined with the white fence and gnarled tree, create a picture symbolic of the smaller homes of America.

FIG. 2-26. Joseph Atwood house, Chatham, Massachusetts. Early American version built on Cape Cod. Gambrel roof and central chimney. Transitional period between seventeenth and eighteenth centuries revealed in more elaborate doorway.

FIG. 2-27. Fireplace and stairway in kitchen of Atwood house. Simple molded shelf over fireplace opening. Wide paneling seen at left. Ceiling now plastered between beams.

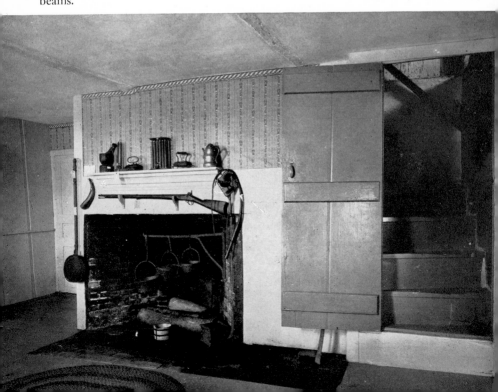

Chapter 3

GEORGIAN PROSPERITY

THE NEW ARISTOCRACY

As the seventeenth century faded into the eighteenth, gradual but conspicuous changes took place in the social environment of the New England colonies. The free land beyond the frontiers challenged the restless and the adventurous but the opportunities for the development of the Atlantic seaboard quickened the imagination of those willing to leave westward migration to the more curious. Thus some chose to go west; others decided to remain in the east.

The latter group carried on with the building of a comfortable colonial life which repeated many of the qualities of mother England. At first the population was composed chiefly of farmers, shopkeepers, shipowners, and fishermen who lived simple lives and built unpretentious houses. However, with the speculation in land and the trading of fish, whale oil, and lumber with countries across the sea for Negroes, mahogany, and rum, there developed an aristocracy in the middle class based upon financial attainments. The representatives of this new colonial aristocracy accumulated the wealth and gained the influence frowned upon by the Puritans a century earlier. They lived as prosperously as did many of their English cousins abroad. They copied English dress, architecture, furniture, and customs. These colonial ladies and gentlemen attired themselves in satins and laces instead of the drab homespun of earlier generations. They ate good food and drank vintage wines served by liveried servants. There was a new social order composed of definitely defined upper and lower classes.

As colonial America grew into maturity and as specialization developed in the larger towns and cities, the self-sufficient household began to move westward with the shifting frontier and to disappear along the eastern seaboard. The clergyman, doctor, merchant, and shipbuilder were the first specialists in the community life. They were joined by the artisans who worked in wood, metal, and leather—artisans who made shoes and saddles and repaired pots and pans, artisans who served as blacksmiths, tailors, and carpenters. Still others manned the mills which were driven by water power for the manufacture of many objects for the home and the shop. Thus the work of both the husband and the wife was made easier; there was more time for the creative household tasks and for the specialized occupational activity of the breadwinner. Such work as weaving, furniture-making, and education—once carried on around the fireplace—was taken outside the home and, as a result, family life and domestic architecture received the direct benefits of changing social and economic conditions.

The meetinghouse continued to be the scene of the social and spiritual life of the New England colonies during most of the eighteenth century. Here the people gathered for Sunday services and weekday lectures even as significant changes were taking place in the religion of the colonists. The English church did not have a monopoly on the souls of men; the Scotch, Dutch, Lutherans, and Irish-Presbyterians were gaining a foothold in the new country. The intolerance of the Puritans was on the defensive, and growing enlightenment was encouraging the development of a more liberal and tolerant point of view. These changes were reflected in the homes which people built, the furnishings they purchased, and the clothing they wore, which would not have been thought of or permitted under the restraining influences of earlier philosophies and spiritual attitudes.

Music in the form of psalm singing was allowed in the churches and was carried outside into other religious and secular activities. Public concerts became popular and competed, at intervals, with the sewing bees and other amusements. Four-page newspapers began to appear, carrying news from Europe and distant colonies, together with sermons and advertisements. However, the village tavern was destined to be the chief source of information and scene for the exchange of ideas and social intercourse. Roads and trails were so few and so poor in the seventeenth century that travel was restricted

FIG. 3-1. Here is one of the outstanding taverns of Colonial America, the Raleigh Tavern, Williamsburg, Virginia. It was the center of the colony's commercial, political, and social life, as were other taverns in the Tidewater region, in the Massachusetts settlements, or along the rocky coast of Maine.

to trips which were absolutely necessary; there was not much incentive for a person to set himself up as an inn-keeper. With the gradual improvements in travel during the eighteenth century, the tavern in eastern colonial America became an important cog in the life of the community, whether located in Massachusetts or Virginia. The tavern was significant in a social sense and equally significant architecturally, since it was domestic in character and resembled the larger homes adjacent to it on the village green or the principal street (Fig. 3-1).

NEW ENGLAND VILLAGES

The Pilgrim and Puritan colonists had belonged primarily to the soil but, with the beginning of the eighteenth century, many of their descendants turned to the sea and to trade. This specialization led to diversification of effort and encouraged the development of communities with various types of people and occupations. By a stroke of good luck, by a favorable trading trip to foreign ports, or by the establishment of a lucrative business, some families prospered more than others. Thus the earlier communal villages were gradually changed into busy commercial towns, and the matter of class based upon difference in wealth and occupation came into sharp focus. The early settlers had lived alike in crude huts or in simple homes of medieval character, but now the larger and more elaborate homes of the well-to-do began to stand out against the background of the modest homes of the poor.

In addition to the efforts of the colonists themselves, other events beyond the Atlantic operated to promote greater prosperity in New England. The Treaty of Utrecht brought about a period of peace which encouraged shipping and commerce. Furniture, clothing, tools, silks, books, and jewelry were sent to America in return for the raw products of this new country. The architecture of eighteenth-century New England flourished in an atmosphere of economic prosperity. The new aristocracy of merchants and shipowners was eager to live well and build beautifully. Handsome homes of wood and brick were erected as a setting for the new social life of the colonies; a spirit of change and progress was in the air. Whereas the Early American home of the seventeenth century came from the soul of man—a soul nurtured by medieval thought and action and by the art and architecture of the Gothic movement—the Georgian homes of the eighteenth century came from the printed page, from the spirit of the Renaissance as portrayed by the drawings of Vignola and Palladio and first interpreted in the manor houses of royal England.

The publication of books on architecture encouraged the creative activities of the amateur architect. Armed with drawings of Renaissance entrances, columns, and entablatures, the gentleman architect and the skilled carpenter designed and built Colonial homes in the Georgian manner. Thus the architecture of England, pictured so well in these books and remembered so vividly by those who journeyed to London on business and pleasure trips, was transplanted to this country. All this was possible through closer association with Europe. With better navigation, with the renunciation of the rigid moral code of seventeenth-century Calvinism, with the development of a higher type of artistic expression, with the importation of beautiful clothes and furniture requiring a proper setting—in short, with the wealth of inspiration and encouragement which accompanied the improved social and economic conditions of the eighteenth century, the art and architecture of Europe found an eager acceptance in America.

However, the change from the medieval to the Georgian was one of gradual growth. The early homes of the eighteenth century retained the simple massing of the seventeenth-century houses and also their type of fenestration. The changes were generally related to better interior planning and to the increased use of decorative forms. Pilasters, columns, cornices, and molded window and door frames became conspicuous features. The greatest changes took place in the towns and cities where the social requirements of the wealthy called for a visual expression of their importance in the community. The simpler forms of exterior massing, or arrangement of major parts, and of architectural details continued in the rural districts and villages well into the nineteenth century.

When the Georgian style was transplanted from England to America, it found a plentiful material waiting for its interpretation. In England, the houses were built of brick and stone; and, while these materials were used in this country for churches, meeting halls, and some of the later and more pretentious homes, the native and indigenous material was wood from the adjacent forests. This use of wood led eventually to a new version of the Renaissance—a version which recognized the limitations and, at the same time, the possibilities of wood. Even though some of these early builders worked with the books of Palladio, while others bent to the influence of Sir Christopher Wren and Inigo Jones, they all managed to give a new and different quality to domestic architecture. The character of Puritan New England could not be discarded overnight and something of the simple idealism and stern regard for honesty remained to color and modify many of the foreign importations. The ornateness of the Georgian from England was, at times, interpreted in wood with a sensitiveness which gave us the beautiful proportions and delicate moldings of the New England Colonial.

Chapter 4

HOUSES FROM HANDBOOKS

EACH summer the inland and coastal towns of New England beckon to the tourist and the vacationist. This attraction is due to a delightful climate, a beautiful scenery of mountains and seashore, and a constant panorama of charming villages. In these villages are still preserved many fine examples of the homes built during the eighteenth century when the American Georgian version of Colonial architecture was at its height. In these homes, built from about the second quarter of the eighteenth century to the time of the Revolutionary War, we may read a history of New England during its most romantic period—a history of the wealthy merchant with his pretentious residence and of the farmer with his more humble but often equally pleasing house. Together they formed the pattern of life during those early years, but too often today we notice only the more familiar and important buildings and overlook the charming homes of less historical and architectural interest. In this discussion we shall try to present representative examples of each type.

THE INSPIRATION

The widespread use of handbooks had a unifying effect upon the domestic architecture of the colonies. There was naturally some difference in the use of materials and in the plans of the houses as they were influenced by climate and the regional social order; but there was, nevertheless, a similarity in the general character and treatment. In the larger and more important buildings there was likely to be an academic quality or a feeling of scholarly research into the historical backgrounds of development and consequently

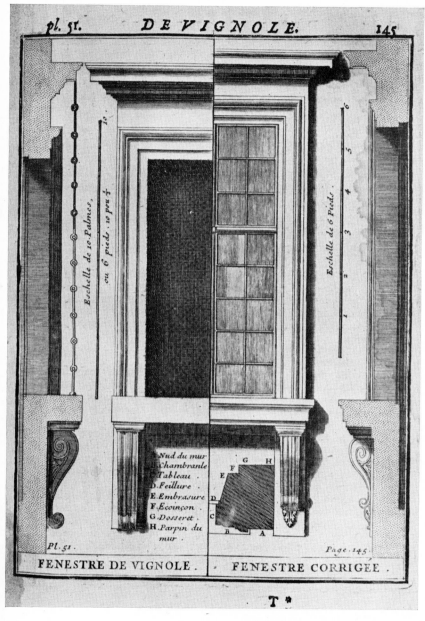

Fig. 4-1. Drawing of a window from "Cours d' Architecture," published in Paris in 1710. This book shows the orders of architecture by Vignola, and the window illustrated may have served as a guide for colonial builders.

a resulting perfection in traditional proportions and treatment. In the smaller and less significant houses, there was often greater freedom in massing and in the use of exterior details, probably because of less dependence upon the use of books and more upon the ingenuity of the carpenter.

It is not surprising that the printed page played such an important part in the design of eighteenth-century Colonial houses. There were, of course, many fine private libraries among the well-to-do families of New England. The books on architecture were well illustrated with copper engravings; the works of Vignola, Palladio, Benjamin, Gibbs, and others were popular and were consulted constantly by the architects and builders of the colonies. In spite of the use of wood, the proportions of architectural motifs provided by handbooks were not altered as much as tradition would have us believe. Although there is evidence of some freedom of expression, the proportions of the architectural details of Renaissance examples were often reproduced in the homes of colonial New England with faithful exactness.

In addition to the popular and widely consulted documents (see Fig. 4-1), there were many books of lesser importance in a scholarly way but of more significance in the encouragement of the carpenter-designer. These handbooks on carpentry and bricklaying, with their illustrations of columns, doors, windows, cornices, and pediments, permitted the intelligent workman to produce a type of architecture that was both logical and beautiful. The scope of these books is indicated by the titles, some of which are *Practical Architecture, The Builder's Dictionary, The American Builder's Companion, Young Carpenter's Assistant*, and others of similar nature. Thus the printed page collaborated with human cleverness and honest expression to produce the most important and perhaps the most charming period of domestic architecture in the history of American growth and development.

CHANGES IN PLAN

The fundamental changes which gradually took place as the Colonial home developed from the Early American dwelling are reflected in the house plans of New England. The earlier plan with

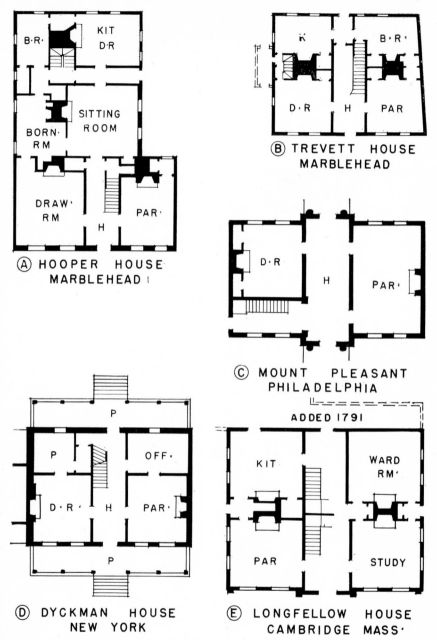

FIG. 4-2. Typical floor plans of houses in the New England and Middle Atlantic colonies. All have center-hall arrangements, with fireplaces between rooms or at ends of building.

the central chimney and cramped stairway, as in the Fisher-Whiting house, Dedham (Fig. 4-11), persisted until well into the eighteenth century; in fact, it was not until about 1750 that the center hall, which carried entirely through the house on the first floor, came into prominence. The Early American houses had been designed with an eye toward maximum utility and economy of materials. However, colonial life in the eighteenth century featured more of the social graces. Greater attention was paid to etiquette, dress, and furnishings; Georgian houses soon felt the influence of a more gracious manner of life. The exteriors of the homes were beautifully decorated and all of the details received a polish and refinement which was lacking in the earlier examples. The central hall, with the improved circulation and cross ventilation which accompanied it, was one of the concessions made to better planning.

The plan of the Longfellow house, Cambridge, shown in Fig. 4-2, is characteristic of the houses of the last half of the eighteenth century. The small entry, or porch, has been replaced by a spacious center hall. This arrangement was achieved by removing the central chimney and substituting two chimneys, one on each side of the hall between the two major rooms of each half of the house. Thus each of the four rooms on each floor was served by its own fireplace. Later the chimneys were moved still farther to the side until they formed part of the end walls against which the ridge of the roof terminated. Thus the chimney lost its structural significance, as in the Samuel Trevett house, Marblehead, Massachusetts, Fig. 4-13, and gave way to the stairway as the important utilitarian and decorative feature. This stairway was usually located at one side of the hall and occupied a position midway between the front and rear entrances. In later examples, the stairway was placed in a separate unit opening into the hall from one side which permitted a more open treatment of the hall itself without the interference of this element of vertical circulation.

The Longfellow house was built in 1759 by Major John Vassall, occupied by General Washington in 1775-1776, and enlarged by Andrew Craigie in 1793. Longfellow lived here from 1837 to 1882. The plan in Fig. 4-2 shows its original size and its use by Washington. Craigie added the two piazzas shown in Fig. 4-3 and an ell at the back which contained the kitchen and other services. The original kitchen

FIG. 4-3. Longfellow house, Cambridge, Massachusetts. Built in 1759. Facade ornamented with four white Ionic pilasters. Hipped roof with balustrade. Once occupied by General Washington. Plan in Fig. 4-2.

FIG. 4-4. Ropes Memorial, Salem, Massachusetts. A typical eighteenth-century Colonial house. Engaged Ionic columns at entrance, harmonizing gateposts. Balustrade on roof suggests captain's walk.

became the dining room, and Washington's ward room was enlargeu into the library.

The rooms on the first floor of the New England Colonial house varied somewhat in name and function with the different examples and periods but, in general, they may be identified as parlor, sitting room, "hall," dining room, kitchen, or bedroom. In many instances the kitchen with its dependencies was located in a rear ell which was sometimes one story in height. This ell, projecting toward the rear, was, no doubt, the forerunner of the sheds, barns, and other servic' units that were attached to farmhouses in one continuous line, as ii the example shown in Fig. P-15, to afford protection from the severe winters of New England. The room in the rear corner of the mair part of the house adjacent to the kitchen was the dining room, while in front of the latter was the "hall," or living room. On the other side of the hall was the drawing room, behind which was a chamber or bedroom.

In the homes of the center-hall type the second floor repeated the plan arrangement of the first floor. The attic space under the lean-to roof at the rear of the Early American house gave way to a full second floor over the rooms which had formerly been located behind the central chimney. The ridge of the roof thus moved back to center over the new and enlarged exterior composition. The sleeping room on the first floor was the only one designated as a bedroom —the other rooms assigned to this purpose on the second floor were always known as chambers, and each was identified by the function and name of the room immediately under it on the first floor.

The center-hall type of house plan persisted for many generations and even today is modified in the so-called Colonial examples largely by the development of a large living room on one side of the hall, with the two rooms on the other side retaining their use as the kitchen and dining room. It was not until the nineteenth century brought the Greek Revival movement that this type of plan lost some of its popularity. Classical architecture dictated a different direction for the main axis of the house. The Georgian house turned its longer dimension and its roof ridge parallel to the street, but the Greek temple with its portico at the end of the building created a new arrangement.

One of the chief differences between an Early American house nd an eighteenth-century Colonial was an improved plan arrangement which permitted better circulation, greater comfort, and more privacy. After the frontiers were pushed westward, the rigorous climate understood and prepared for, and the economic status of the people improved to permit additional leisure time for the amenities of life, greater attention was paid to planning for convenience. The kitchen was no longer used for working, dining, entertaining, and sleeping; there was a greater separation of basic family activities. The situation was somewhat analogous to a family living in a present-day tenement where the entire family and all its domestic activities are crowded into one or two rooms. Upon removal to a modern, subsidized housing development, the family finds separate rooms for cooking, dining, relaxing, and sleeping. Changing social conditions demanded a similar separation of activities during the eighteenth century, and rooms were created for various domestic functions. In the Georgian Colonial homes there was also a conscious effort to plan for greater ease of circulation by means of properly placed doors and by the use of halls and stairways. Rooms could thus be reached directly instead of by passage through other rooms; privacy was thereby attained.

EXTERIOR TREATMENT

For the benefit of those who may not be familiar with the vocabulary of architectural details, especially the details belonging to the Renaissance style of which the various manifestations of the Colonial are a part, the drawing in Fig. 4-5 is presented as a guide. Here are shown the major elements of an entrance, an arched window, and the cornice of a house, together with an identification of the component parts. Here a Doric order is used for the general treatment, with the introduction of an unrelated Ionic pilaster and entablature on the left of the composition for the purpose of showing a variety of forms.

The houses built in New England during the eighteenth century, as well as those constructed in the Middle and South Atlantic colonies, were predominantly symmetrical in plan and exterior treatment. There were, of course, a number of variations and exceptions to this practice, but, in general, Colonial architecture was an orderly

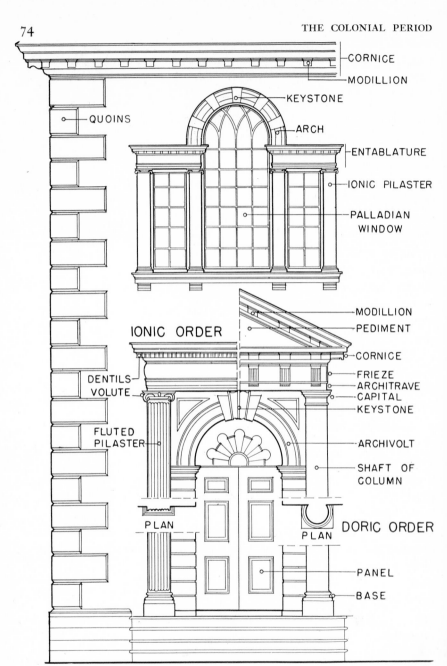

CORNICE

MODILLION

KEYSTONE

QUOINS

ARCH

ENTABLATURE

IONIC PILASTER

PALLADIAN
WINDOW

IONIC ORDER

MODILLION
PEDIMENT

CORNICE
FRIEZE
ARCHITRAVE
CAPITAL
KEYSTONE

DENTILS
VOLUTE

FLUTED
PILASTER

ARCHIVOLT

SHAFT OF
COLUMN

PLAN

PLAN

DORIC ORDER

PANEL

BASE

Fig. 4-5. The decorative elements of Georgian architecture. Except for Ionic insert on left, this drawing is based on the east entrance of Mount Pleasant, Philadelphia. See Fig. 6-23.

and dignified style. The chief architectural feature of the main facade was the centrally located doorway, which was flanked on either side by two windows on the first floor. The fenestration of the second floor repeated that of the first in spacing and regularity. Above the entrance was a window similar to those adjacent—or an accented one in later examples. A cornice, which varied in its richness of detail according to the period in which the house was built, was the crowning feature of the wall.

The wall covering of the early houses consisted of clapboards of oak which were split by hand from the abundant logs so close at hand. Each piece was wedge shaped in section because of the manner of splitting the boards radially from the center of the log. This type of siding was nailed directly to the vertical studs and the boards were lapped to make joints which were weather tight and waterproof. Later it was found that white pine lumber could be worked more easily and was more durable than oak. The pine clapboards and weather boarding were sawed instead of split and were again applied directly to the studs. In the later houses the lower edge of each board was finished with a beaded molding which gave an added decorative quality to the wall. In some parts of New England, shingles were used as a wall covering but the familiar wood siding is a more conspicuous and common feature.

In some of the more pretentious homes, such as the Hooper house in Marblehead (Fig. 4-6), there was an attempt to imitate stonework in the use of the siding. The boards were applied flat so that they were flush with each other and they were given beveled edges to simulate masonry joints. In addition, the corners of the house were finished with quoins or raised blocks of wood painted a different color to give the appearance of stone quoins so typical of the masonry architecture of Georgian England, as in the Hooper house (Fig. 4-6). The Hooper mansion was built in 1745 by the merchant prince and shipowner, "Robert Hooper, Esquire," nicknamed "King" because of his scale of living and his integrity in dealing with his sailors. The formal main facade, with its fine cornice, screens an informal, five-story wing in the rear, as indicated in Fig. 4-2. On the top floor of the front unit is the banquet hall with delicate vaulting where "King" Hooper held his royal entertainments.

Colonial doorways followed the pattern set by the general character of the house itself. In the early and unpretentious examples, the entrance was a simple opening framed by a plain casing and enclosing an equally plain door of boards. In the development of the doorway, one of the first changes was the introduction of a door with panels and the use of moldings around the frame. A glazed transom, which later became a decorative feature, was also added as a utilitarian device for furnishing the only natural illumination for the entry.

However, the beauty and elegance of Georgian architecture was not to be denied for long. The architect or builder, armed with handbooks, experimented with the more ornate forms of Renaissance details; the doorway with plain or fluted pilasters on either side of the opening began to appear. The pilasters carried an entablature which was treated in one of several ways. In some cases the entablature consisted of the typical combination of horizontal members— the architrave, frieze, and cornice (illustrated in Fig. 4-5). An example of this simple type is shown in the entrance of the Captain Samuel Trevett house, Marblehead, Massachusetts, Fig. 4-13. Here Doric pilasters carry a plain entablature, the cornice of which is similar to the cornices appearing over the windows on the first floor.

Another variation in the treatment of the doorway was the use of a pediment as the crowning feature of the composition. The Captain John Stearns house at Oldtown, Massachusetts, Fig. 4-7, illustrates the use of this characteristic architectural feature. However, here the treatment under the pediment is somewhat unusual and more ornate than customary. The transom light breaks through into the space reserved for the architrave and frieze and thus gives an added decorative quality to the arrangement.

In other examples, the pediment is curved, as in the entrance to the Knight-Short house, Newbury, Massachusetts, Fig. 4-8, while in still others the moldings of the pediment are broken into reverse curves terminating in rosettes.

Later types of Colonial entrances are shown in the Monroe house, South Shaftsbury, Vermont, Fig. 4-9, and the Hull Sherwood house, Fairfield, Connecticut, Fig. 4-10. In the former example, slender coupled columns occur on each side of the opening and are combined with a semicircular fanlight which breaks into the space below the pediment. In the latter example a porch protects the entrance and provides added shelter from the weather. Those entrances, with

FIG. 4-6. Robert "King" Hooper house, Marblehead, Massachusetts. Built in 1745. Monumental mansion of frame construction simulating stone. Note quoins at corner. This was the town house of a merchant prince and shipowner, its Classical facade worthy of this honor. Plan in Fig. 4-2.

engaged or freestanding columns, semielliptical or semicircular fan-
lights of leaded glass, elaborate side lights, gabled roofs, and other
decorative features, usually belong to the late Colonial period. Their
character is the result of the Georgian influence as it climaxed its
transition into the Post-Colonial or Federal style of the early nineteenth century.

As the Colonial style developed during the eighteenth century,
the windows became regular in spacing and important in size. The
small casement windows of the Early American period gave way to
the double-hung windows of the Georgian. The rectangular panes
of glass determined the size and proportions of the window sash. In
the early houses there was an unequal number of lights between the
two sashes; in some instances the upper sash was two panes high and
the lower was three, in others the count was reversed. It is in the
later examples that the sash were of equal size. The modern double-
hung window with counter weights or springs was unknown to
Colonial builders. These builders fixed the upper sash in place and
operated only the lower one by sliding it up and down.

While a number of the Colonial houses had windows with little
architectural adornment, many typical examples showed the use of
a molded frame often used alone but frequently surmounted by a
horizontal cornice or a pediment. Windows with the simplest type
of molded trim are shown in the General William Brattle house, Fig.
4-15, the Hull Sherwood house, Fig. 4-19, and the Longfellow house,
Fig. 4-3. In the Captain Samuel Trevett house, Fig. 4-13, is to be seen
the use of windows with complete entablatures. Windows were
usually uniformly treated across the entire facade unless the one over
the entrance received special attention and accentuation. This variation above the doorway often assumed the form of a Palladian window, which may be seen in the Monroe house, Fig. 4-18. The
presence of this type of window indicates the late date of the house,
since this elegant and graceful treatment generally belonged to the
Post-Colonial or Federal period of the early nineteenth century.

The cornice was the crowning feature of the exterior wall and
varied in character with the wealth of the owner, the importance
of the building, and the date of construction. Fundamentally the
cornice is the extension of the ceiling joist of the top floor beyond
the face of the wall to form a protecting overhang. From this over-

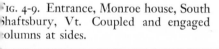

Fig. 4-7. Entrance, Stearns house, Old-own, Mass. Fluted Doric pilasters.

Fig. 4-8. Entrance, Knight-Short house, Newbury, Mass. Curved pediment.

Fig. 4-9. Entrance, Monroe house, South Shaftsbury, Vt. Coupled and engaged columns at sides.

Fig. 4-10. Entrance, Hull Sherwood house, Fairfield, Conn. Transom and sidelight windows.

FIG. 4-11. Fisher-Whiting house, Dedham, Massachusetts. 1669. Colonial exterior later. Plan in Fig. 2-2.

FIG. 4-12. Simple treatment of dining room wall shows early date.

4-13. Captain Samuel Trevett house, Marblehead, Massachusetts. Mid eighteenth ~~ry. Typical center-hall type permitted by two chimneys instead of Early Ameri-central chimney. Symmetrical facade. Entrance and windows have complete ~~latures. Plan in Fig. 4-2.

4-14. Fireplace wall in first-floor room, Trevett house. Note simple paneling in ~s and wall, also absence of shelf over fireplace opening. Note wide floor boards.

FIG. 4-15. General William Brattle house, Cambridge, Massachusetts, dates back to early eighteenth century. It has a gambrel roof with dormers, bracketed cornice, and symmetrically spaced windows. The projecting entrance has Doric pilasters, entablature and pediment.

FIG. 4-16. Interior of first-floor room, showing elaborate wall treatment with fluted pilasters and overmantel with ears. Curved panels in door are unusual.

Fig. 4-17. Captain John Stearns house, Oldtown, Massachusetts. Central chimney indicates early date but exterior treatment is typically Colonial. Pedimented doorway is shown in Fig. 4-7.

hang the roof slopes backward to the ridge and completes the exterior composition of the house. The ends of the joist and roof rafters, in Colonial or in modern derivations thereof, are enclosed or cased on the face and the bottom with boards and finished with simple ogee, or S-shaped, moldings. This type of cornice is illustrated in the Captain John Stearns house, Fig. 4-17. In later structures, dentil courses and modillion brackets, Fig. 4-5, together with other Renaissance decorations, were added to the cornice, as in the Brattle house, Fig. 4-15, and the Hooper house, Fig. 4-6.

As the Colonial style became of age and merged with the Post-Colonial of the early nineteenth century, the cornice developed into the full-fledged entablature complete with frieze, architrave, and cornice—all expressed according to the simplicity of the Doric order, the gracefulness of the Ionic, or the richness of the Corinthian. The Longfellow house, in Cambridge, shown in Fig. 4-3, employed the full entablature over the pilasters but we must turn to later examples for illustrations of its most complete use. The Longfellow house also

FIG. 4-18. Monroe house, South Shaftsbury, Vermont. Paneled Ionic pilasters, elaborate entablature, and Palladian window with pediment indicate late eighteenth-century treatment. Pedimented entrance is shown in Fig. 4-9.

FIG. 4-19. Hull Sherwood house, Fairfield, Connecticut. Built in 1816. An indication of how Colonial treatment carried into nineteenth century.

Fig. 4-20. House at East Sullivan, Maine. Refined Colonial treatment typical of early nineteenth-century architecture. Forerunner of Post-Colonial.

shows the manner in which pilasters were used at the corners of the house—and, in this case, at the entrance—to give an added feeling of formality to the facade. This house also serves as an illustration of the method of carrying the cornice around the four facades of those houses with hipped roofs. In most dwellings with gable roofs, the cornice was returned against the front elevation or against the end walls just around the corner from the main facade. It is only in the later examples that the cornice carried across the gable ends, as in the Monroe house, Fig. 4-18.

The roofs of the eighteenth-century houses were usually not as steep as those of the preceding century. In the majority of Colonial houses, especially those modest in size, the roof terminated in a ridge parallel with the front facade; in the later and larger houses, the roofs were surmounted by a balustrade, a captain's walk, or a cupola. The Jeremiah Lee house in Marblehead has a cupola, while the Longfellow house, Fig. 4-3, and the Ropes Memorial, Fig. 4-4, have balustrades. Except for those roofs which were hipped, roofs usually consisted of two planes, or slopes, with a simple gable at either end. In some instances, however, the gambrel roof was employed. This means that there were four slopes or planes instead of two, as shown in the Brattle house, Fig. 4-15. This house also illustrates the use of dormer windows as conspicuous features of the roof, which provide an extra decorative note to the exterior composition. The dormers, when employed, were usually spaced symmetrically with reference to the second-floor windows. Their general direction was vertical and they were treated with molded trim and plain or curved pediments.

INTERIOR BEAUTY

The interiors of the Colonial houses of the eighteenth century usually reflected the character of the exteriors, both of which developed slowly in ornateness and richness as the century progressed. It must be remembered that these Colonial builders were often direct descendants of the Puritans and Pilgrims and that acceptance of even mild degrees of ostentation in the design of homes was a gradual process. The movement began with the use of paneled doors and walls, simple wainscots, and decorative mantels for the fireplaces, and led to the more ornate forms of the various architectural motifs. Thus there was a slow transition from the simplicity of the early part of the century to the richness of the last part.

It is difficult to write accurately about the floors of the homes of the Colonial period because, in spite of the fact that they were probably made of oak, the wear of generations of occupants makes it probable that little of the original boards are left. It is reasonably certain, however, that oak was succeeded by hard pine and that the boards were laid down in random widths. The first-floor rooms usually had double floors while a single floor seemed to be considered adequate for the second floor. In the finer homes of the late eighteenth century, marquetry, or floors of fine woods laid in geometrical patterns, became the fashion.

As we enter a typical Colonial house, immediately ahead of us is a spacious hall with a richly decorated stairway instead of the seventeenth-century narrow entry with its steep, winding stairs. On this eighteenth-century stairway, designers lavished much care and attention; this feature of the house was important by reason of both location and treatment. The stairway usually began with a

FIGS. 4-21 and 4-22. Two views of the elaborate stairway in the Hooper house, one of the finest in colonial America, showing the paneled ends of steps and spiral balusters and newel. Example of the fine craftsmanship of the period.

decorative newel post, which was the terminus of a beautifully carved balustrade composed of turned spindles, or of those of the twisted or rope pattern, together with a molded handrail of mahogany or walnut. There was naturally a change in the character of the balusters or spindles as the century progressed. They became more slender, longer, and more ornately carved and turned. In some cases the turning was around the baluster in a horizontal direction but in many the spiral direction was followed and the rope type developed. The newel posts likewise followed the fashion by departing from the early square form and progressing through the various stages to the type in which the balustrade was wrapped around the newel to form a volute, similar to that in Fig. 4-22.

The richness of a typical stairway is illustrated in the view of the hallway of the Hooper house, in Marblehead. In this example there is a display of another characteristic, which is the use of the open string allowing the treads to extend beyond the line of balusters.

This permitted the decorative scroll-shaped brackets, used in connection with the paneled ends, to be a conspicuous feature of the composition. This type of stairway was far removed from the simple character of the earlier examples in which the ends were closed and balusters rested directly on the facia board, as in Fig. 2-21.

The wall treatment of the major rooms of the Colonial house varied with the size and character of the house itself. In the early houses of the seventeenth century the walls were covered with pine boards but later this type of paneling gave way to the use of plaster. This practice did not eliminate wood as a decorative material since it was necessary to use a baseboard as a transition between the wall and the floor, a chair rail at the proper height on the wall, and also a simple cornice or set of moldings at the intersection of the wall and ceiling. By the middle of the eighteenth century, the fireplace walls of the major rooms in the Colonial house were paneled in a manner similar to that shown in the Trevett house, Fig. 4-14. Here, as was often the case elsewhere, this side of the room was composed of rectangular panels with simple moldings, panels which were vertical on either side of the fireplace and horizontal above. In later houses the paneling became more elaborate; fluted pilasters with a complete cornice were sometimes used, and the area between was filled with panels with curved heads to form a rich composition characteristic of the late phases of the Georgian, as in Fig. 4-16.

In many of the old houses of New England there is evidence of the popularity of wallpaper which was imported from England and France. These highly decorative papers usually depicted landscapes and historical events and were applied to the walls above the wainscots of the stairway and in the major rooms of the house. This suggests that the rooms of the houses of Colonial New England were more colorful than present-day interpretations would have us believe. Unfortunately the eclectic period of the early part of the twentieth century endowed current Colonial interiors with a sterility of white enamel which is contrary to the richness of eighteenth-century Colonial. The restoration of the Georgian buildings at Williamsburg has given us a pleasant and accurate insight into the charm of the interiors of two centuries ago. In much of the old domestic architecture of the Atlantic seaboard, the woodwork and walls were painted in pastel tones of blue, gray, green, or dull red. These colors were repeated in the chintzes, damasks, and other fabrics of the upholstering and the hangings, giving to the interiors a sparkle of gaiety in tune with the balls and dinners of this romantic period.

The beautiful interior doorways of Colonial houses—doorways through which passed generations of ladies and gentlemen in their silks and satins and servants and retainers in their homespun—varied from the simple square-headed type with moldings mitered at the corners to the more ornate with pediments of the regular, curved, or broken variety. In addition, arched doorways, either semicircular or three-centered in type, are to be found in many of the homes built during the last part of the eighteenth century. In the early part of the century there was some modification of Classical proportions in recognition of the nature of wood but extreme attenuation and delicacy did not become conspicuous until the influence of the Adam style, which by date was related to the beginning of the nineteenth century. The doors themselves developed in complexity with the growth of the Colonial style. The simple batten doors of the Early American period gave way to the earliest forms of the paneled type with only two or three panels. Later examples showed the use of four and six panels, illustrated in the Fisher-Whiting house in Dedham, Fig. 4-12.

We have reserved for the last a description of the most important architectural feature of the main rooms of the house, namely the fireplace and its accompanying mantel. Here the designer developed a focal point or center of interest which set the style for the remainder of the interior treatment. Here the designer created exquisite compositions of moldings and carving which revealed the economic, social, and artistic progress of the colonists, whether they were English, Dutch, or German. The fireplace with which the designer worked consisted of the hearth, or firebox, itself built of brick, its decorative facing of brick or marble, and the surrounding wooden treatment of moldings, shelf, panels, pilasters, and columns, used in varying combinations. The wood trim around the fireplace opening usually followed the pattern of one of two general types. In one type the masonry construction and the mantel projected beyond the face of the wall and carried upward to the ceiling; in the other, the fireplace treatment was flush with the surrounding wall.

In early examples, the general composition and details of the fireplace were simple in design and character. In some instances the opening was surrounded with moldings mitered at the corners, and in

others, as in the Trevett house, Fig. 4-14, the opening was unadorne
except for the paneling of the wall. Mantels without shelves remai
popular for several decades or until the influence of the richer
later Georgian treatment began to be felt. Perhaps the first step aw
from the early simplicity was the introduction of "ears," or projections, at the two upper corners of the opening. This led to the use
of other decorative features and paved the way for a complete sur-
render to the richness of the late Colonial style.

The next step in the development of the fireplace resulted in the
use of pilasters—one on either side of the opening—which in turn supported an entablature. Usually the proportions of the moldings of
the various members of the composition were adjusted to the properties of the wood from which the mantels were constructed. A degree of delicacy and attenuation was attained which would have been
difficult with the use of stone. An example of this is the exaggerated
projection of the cornice to form the shelf or the crowning feature
of the entire composition. The fireplace in the Brattle house, Fig.
4-16, shows the use of the pilastered mantel surmounted by the paneled overmantel with "ears." In this example there are pilasters which
frame the treatment and give a dignity and importance typical of
the best work of the late period.

As the century progressed and the architectural treatment of the
exterior and interior became more ornate, the mantels of the major
rooms of the house became more elaborate in design. This was especially true of the mantelpiece in the parlor, which received th
most attention. The living room mantel was usually less complex
treatment while the mantels of the bedrooms on the second floor wei
even less pretentious. The later examples were embellished by engaged columns used in pairs on either side of the opening, by the
friezes carved with festoons and figures, and by elaborate overmantels
composed of pilasters, panels, and broken pediments.

The fireplaces, like the stairways, do much to reveal the historica
date of a house. On these conspicuous features the skillful designers
and clever craftsmen lavished their loving care; here was told the
current story of architectural practice. Whether simple pine boards
and crude moldings or painted woodwork and delicate cornices were
used, these beautiful and significant accents in Colonial interiors reveal the attitudes and tastes of the various periods. The simplicity of

the Early American, the delicacy of the transitional Colonial, or the richness of the Georgian is dramatically symbolized by the treatment of the stairway and the fireplace.

It would have been very incongruous if the furniture used during the Colonial days had not followed the same general pattern of development and change as the architecture of the eighteenth century. This is true in the homes of the farmer and the villager, as well as in those of the wealthy shipowner and merchant. In the more humble homes of the colonies, the architectural treatment of the interiors retained a simplicity which often bordered on the primitive; it is, therefore, natural that the plain furniture of Early American origin continued to satisfy the needs of those lower in the social and economic scale. However, the more formal homes of Boston, Salem, and Portsmouth provided a setting which, together with the demands of an aristocratic existence, called for the products of the skilled cabinetmakers of the colonies and England. This was the age of beautiful joinery and woodworking on both sides of the ocean; and, as a result, handsome chairs, tables, chests, highboys, and desks were created in the manner of the Queen Anne, Sheraton, and Hepplewhite styles. Mahogany was imported for many of the magnificent pieces; in addition, such native woods as maple, cherry, and walnut were popular.

It hardly seems necessary to describe a Colonial room of the eighteenth century, since there have been so many restorations and reproductions. Needless to say, these interiors had a charm and beauty which has not been surpassed by later decorators and home-makers. The graceful chairs upholstered in calico, damask, or velvet, the lowboys with broken pediments, the gracefully formed sofas, and the richly decorated desks, clocks, beds, and chests all contributed to the successful and colorful compositions with which we are so familiar from actual experience or from words and pictures. If we can illuminate these interiors with the many candles in their candelabra and in the center chandelier, and if we people these rooms with beautiful ladies and gallant gentlemen, we have a scene of true dignity, delicacy, and beauty.

Chapter 5

THE DUTCH, QUAKERS, AND GERMANS

THE HUDSON RIVER VALLEY

WHILE the colonization of the New England area was proceeding at an ever accelerating rate, the Dutch, Quakers, and Germans were moving into the valleys of the Hudson and the Mohawk and westward into the fertile plains of eastern Pennsylvania. This movement had its beginning early in the seventeenth century when the intrepid explorer, Henry Hudson, financed by a group of merchants in Amsterdam, set out to seek a more satisfactory route to India. With high hopes he sailed up the great river which now bears his name, only to find that it was not the highway to the riches of the Orient.

But the Dutch were to learn that wealth is not confined to gold and precious stones. The Oriental treasures for which these Dutch merchants were seeking were not to be reached by way of the Hudson River. However, they were not completely disappointed, for other sources of wealth were revealed to them. They discovered that the skins of the mink, otter, and beaver could be obtained from the Indians of the New World for a few inexpensive ornaments and, as a result, traders soon came in numbers to the mouth of the Hudson. Here the emphasis was upon profitable investments rather than upon religious freedom.

Large grants of land were made to every patroon who could establish a semifeudal estate along the water routes to New Amsterdam. In the rich soil of the river valleys, crops of tobacco, vegetables, and grain were grown for consumption and export. The Dutch settlers had hearty appetites and they stocked their storerooms with pickled pork from their pens, fish from their rivers, and fruit and corn from their gardens. But there was a surplus to be carried by boat to New Amsterdam for shipment abroad. Beaver skins became the accepted form of currency in the back country and, finding their way to the trade routes of Europe, were largely responsible for the development of the town at the mouth of the Hudson into a thriving and bustling community.

However, the industrious traits of the Dutch did not interfere with their joy of living. In addition to their love of good food, they were fond of alcoholic drinks, a trait quite unlike those of their New England neighbors, the Puritans. They believed in sturdy merriment and their weddings, receptions, and parties were festive occasions. This predilection for physical comfort and pleasure was reflected in the houses which they built. Even their early homes exhibited a substantial and sophisticated quality comparable to those in the cities of Holland.

In spite of the organization of the settlements and the frugality and industry of the people, the Dutch were not destined to maintain their supremacy for long. They were too close to the English colonies for the comfort of the followers of Charles II and in 1664 the short-lived empire of New Netherland surrendered to an English fleet. However, this change in government did not bring an immediate change in the social and economic life of the Hudson Valley. Instead, New York assumed an English character quite gradually while Albany and other settlement to the north remained Dutch in architecture and spirit for many years. Even though the English and many of the more wealthy Dutch built Georgian mansions in the New York area, the middle class continued for some time to design and construct houses in the medieval manner so typical of the towns of Holland or in the familiar Dutch Colonial version which has persisted in a modified form even to the present day.

THE PENNSYLVANIA REGION

William Penn was a young Quaker whose devotion to his religious convictions prompted him to look for a sanctuary for the persecuted Society of Friends. When he came into possession of a fortune upon the death of his father in 1670, he turned toward America for both refuge and financial gain. His inheritance included a large tract of land which corresponded roughly to the region now called Pennsylvania. His methods of recruiting settlers from abroad brought to this colony a variety of people, people dominated by the Quakers but composed also of German Protestants, Scotch-Irish Presbyterians, Welsh Baptists, and Irish Catholics. They were, in the main, middle-class merchants and farmers; Pennsylvania, with its equitable climate, inviting topography, and rich soil, became a land of farms and towns instead of a region of estates and manor houses as in the colony of Virginia to the south.

By the beginning of the last half of the eighteenth century, the middle colonies rivaled the New England and tidewater colonies in matters social, economic, and architectural. The middle colonies shared in the prosperity that came to all of the settlements along the Atlantic seaboard, a prosperity that was favorable to the building of homes and the growth of cities. The seaports of Boston, Portsmouth, and Providence saw the development of trade in lumber and fish but the cities of Philadelphia and New York became centers of export for the products of the Hudson Valley and of the Pennsylvania farms.

Philadelphia was the largest city along the Atlantic coast by the middle of the eighteenth century. Its streets were laid out on the gridiron pattern in contrast with the winding lanes of Boston, and these streets were lined with substantial brick or stone houses. While the Quakers, at first, held strictly to their religious convictions and to the simplicity of their existence, they were tolerant toward the more secular diversions of their neighbors. In time, even the Quakers themselves succumbed to the influences of wealth—of living in fine mansions—and their original stand on dress, conduct, and amusement was gradually modified. As a result, Philadelphia became a leader among the larger cities of the country in matters of culture, education, art, and architecture. It was a Renaissance city of elegance and the envy of visitors from abroad. Its economic and social life encouraged the erection of fine Georgian mansions and the furnishing of these homes as a setting for the gatherings of the influential people of the region.

Chapter 6

VARIATIONS OF A THEME

THE DUTCH

In the same manner that the English colonists brought ideas about Georgian architecture to Boston, the Dutch settlers cherished in their new homes of New Amsterdam memories of the houses that they had left behind in Holland. Unfortunately we must depend on old prints for most of the evidence of the town houses that these sturdy Dutch people erected; with the intervening centuries and the inexorable march of progress, these early structures have almost entirely disappeared.

All evidence points to the European character of these Dutch homes. The old prints, such as the one of the Widow Sturtevant house in Albany, Fig. 6-2, show that the typical stepped gable, so characteristic of old Amsterdam, was conspicuous in the early architecture of New York and Albany. The decorated gable ends, the colorful shutters, and the unsymmetrically placed entrance with its high stoop were imported directly with little change from the picturesque streets and squares of the towns of the Low Country.

This influence was maintained in the Hudson River valley for several decades; but, with the pressure of the surrounding English Colonial and with the destruction of these Dutch buildings of brick, another type of architecture came to be representative of the people from Holland. This type was symbolized by simple houses of stone masonry, designed and built in the most direct manner. The houses were long, low, rectilinear structures with plain doors and windows, all of the component parts being arranged in an unsymmetrical com-

95

position terminating with chimneys at either end, Fig. 6-1. Very often the roof finished against the end walls which extended above the roof to form a sloped coping. These houses were so unpretentious architecturally that those which remain today on busy city streets or unimportant country roads usually go unnoticed by all except the avid historian or the eager student of architecture. Some of these simple houses, most of which were built early in the eighteenth century, are illustrated in Figs. 6-3 through 6-7. They exhibit various degrees of New World influence but they have in common the humble stone walls of random stone and a general air of unpretentiousness.

After the early decades, the more popular Dutch Colonial architecture was developed in the region of New York City. This style, which spread for a number of miles into the surrounding territory, had many characteristics in common with the domestic architecture of New England; it varied from the latter style, however, in the composition of its massing and the use of its details. It soon replaced the European buildings of the first settlers and also the simple stone cottages of the transitional period.

This Dutch version of the Colonial—the one that has been handed down in a much modified form for present-day builders—is well illustrated in the Dyckman house, built in 1785, Fig. 6-12. Here is to be seen the typical low-pitched gambrel roof, or the roof with two slopes on each side of the ridge. In most examples of this style, the upper slope is usually about 30 degrees with the horizontal while the lower slope had a pitch of about 45 degrees. As will be seen from the illustration, the lower slope often ended in a sweeping curve that projected beyond the wall far enough to form a porch. The source of the roof projection is to be found in the homes of the mother country, where the Flemish cottages were built of clay which was not impervious to rain. It was imperative that protection be provided and consequently the roof was projected to create the necessary shelter. The overhang carried across the front and the back of the house, which left the ends unprotected. In an attempt to correct this situation, the upper parts of the ends under the gable were covered with shingles or clapboards. The projection of the roof was sometimes wide enough to require the use of slender columns—in other cases its projection was less pronounced and served only as a

Fig. 6-1. Van Alstyne house, Canajoharie, New York. Mid eighteenth century.

Fig. 6-2. Widow Sturtevant house, Albany, New York. Stepped gables.

FIG. 6-3. Hasbrouck house, Newburgh, New York. Was Washington's headquarters. Early eighteenth century.

FIG. 6-4. Entrance, with contrast between delicate moldings and rough stonework.

Fig. 6-5. Jan Mabie house, Rotterdam Junction, New York. 1618-70.

Fig. 6-6. Exterior detail, showing simplicity of treatment.

Fig. 6-7. Jean Hasbrouck house, New Paltz, New York. Early date, 1712, indicated by the steep roof, small windows, and simple character of exterior. The walls are built of field stone except for the gable ends which are of wood to give greater protection from the rain.

Fig. 6-8. Bedroom on first floor. The wide boards of the floor, beamed ceiling, and four-poster bed with canopy blend to create a typical early Colonial interior.

Fig. 6-9. Browne house, Flushing, New York. Built in the seventeenth century, it has the long sloping dormers which were characteristic of the homes built in the early Dutch villages along the Hudson River. Here the walls are of wood rather than the commonly used field stone.

Fig. 6-10. Corner of the dining room, showing sturdy Dutch furniture.

Fig. 6-11. Interior of the front door divided to form popular "Dutch door."

hood. Regardless of the depth of this architectural feature, it provided a shelter under which the sturdy burghers and their families sat on summer evenings to discuss the yield of their crops and the threats of English domination.

The walls of these Dutch Colonial houses were constructed of stone and wood or sometimes entirely of wood. The masonry was reserved for the lower part of the walls and usually consisted of field stone laid with white mortar to form areas of interesting texture and color, a treatment which is generally associated with the domestic architecture of the middle colonies. In those houses with stone walls, the use of wood was confined to the gable ends and to the porches, exterior trim, lower wings, and other minor elements. When the walls were built entirely of wood, the covering material was either horizontal siding or shingles, as in the Browne house, Fig. 6-9.

The plans of these Dutch houses varied in arrangement perhaps more than did those of neighboring colonies. A composition approaching symmetry is to be found in the Dyckman house, Fig. 4-2, but many were quite unsymmetrical in their layout. The interiors usually reflected the sturdy construction and the simple design of the exteriors. The kitchen of the Dyckman house, Fig. 6-13, is typical of most of the earlier homes. Here the customary large fireplace, which held the andirons, racks, spits, kettles, and other utensils, served the same purpose as the fireplace of the New England home. It points to the fact that, in general, colonial life for the Dutch was similar to that for the English, except for those differences that grew from dissimilar backgrounds in Europe and the tenacity with which the resulting traditions were maintained in the New World. Dutch architectural expressions, therefore, did not deviate too much from the established Colonial pattern.

The most pronounced national traits were, perhaps, more vigorously retained in the furniture and the furnishings of the period. In common with the Germans, the Dutch had a warm affection for the heavy, substantial furniture which they knew in the old country, as shown in Fig. 6-10. This simple furniture was combined with pewter, Delft ceramic ware, tile, and glass to create unpretentious but cheerful and homelike rooms entirely in keeping with the character of the occupants of these houses.

Fig. 6-12. Dyckman house, New York. This house, once a typical Dutch farmhouse far out in the country, is preserved as a monument to the sturdy burghers of the Hudson River settlements. It has a gambrel roof with a porch and its walls are built of field stone and clapboards.

Fig. 6-13. Interior view of kitchen, Dyckman house, showing the large fireplace and the cooking utensils in this basement room under the dining room. See plan, Fig. 4-2.

Fig. 6-14. Payne Memorial. East Hampton, New York. Mid seventeenth century. Exterior Early American treatment.

Fig. 6-15. Entrance, showing simple character. Compare with Fig. 2-11.

Fig. 6-16. Corner of the dining room, "Home Sweet Home" house. Payne Memorial.

THE QUAKERS AND GERMANS

While the Dutch Colonial style was lingering on in the New York area, the neighboring territory of New Jersey, Delaware, and Pennsylvania was witnessing the development of a variety of only slightly divergent architectural movements. Here the Quakers, Germans, Scotch, Irish, Welsh, and Swedes were building homes which showed the influence of local building materials and customs upon the various phases of Georgian architecture as the latter crowded in from the surrounding colonies. At times it is difficult to assign definite descriptive terms which will remain unchallenged. Throughout the region, as the English influence became stronger, the early architecture was modified in varying degrees by the nationalistic traits of the settlers. For the sake of a brief approach, the remainder of our discussion of Colonial architecture of the middle colonies may be divided into two parts: one dealing with the simpler houses of the Quakers and the Germans and of those who came under their influence in the area around Philadelphia and to the west, the other with those later and

FIG. 6-17. Steelman house, Pennsauken Township, New Jersey. The projecting hood, or pent roof, across the front above the first-floor windows is typical of the period. House has the same sloping dormers as the Browne house, Fig. 6-9. The walls are of field stone. Date, 1728-1749.

FIG. 6-18. Kitchen fireplace, Steelman house. The architectural treatment corresponds to the exterior with its simple projecting shelf and unpretentious paneling.

Fig. 6-19. A Pennsylvania German farmhouse. An inscription carved on a stone in the front wall reads "Built by Jacob and Sarah Shank, 1836." Here is a typical house of the Lancaster area, the field-stone walls reflecting the simple life of the period.

Fig. 6-20. The front facade of the Shank house, with its deeply recessed door revealing the thickness of the walls. Also shown are the windows with their beautifully paneled shutters. (Photos by Long & York.)

more ambitious homes which showed a stronger predilection for the Classical aspects of the Georgian.

Until the middle of the eighteenth century, when Georgian influence gained the upper hand, the simple, sturdy architecture of the Quakers, so characteristic of the people themselves, was conspicuous in the Philadelphia area. Here and for miles around in the surrounding territory were to be found many examples of stone buildings similar to the Steelman house, illustrated in Fig. 6-17. One of the conspicuous features of these houses was the roofed projection between the windows of the first and second floors. This pent roof was popular in England where it covered a narrow balcony and it was no surprise that the Quakers remembered it when they built their versions of Georgian architecture in this country. It was also common in parts of Germany and it is, therefore, sometimes difficult to distinguish between Quaker and German influence. While this roof was usually carried across the front of the house, it was often used on the ends as a continuation of the cornice, as shown in Wister's Big House, Fig. 6-21. This projecting roof was so common with the houses of Germantown that it is sometimes called the "Germantown hood."

Early in the eighteenth century the German farmers from the Palatinate and the Amish and Mennonites from Switzerland came to the rich, fertile valleys west of Philadelphia. At first, they built simple log houses which were followed by a few in the half-timber style of medieval Europe. However, these early examples have generally vanished, except for such structures as the Klosters at Ephrata; and Pennsylvania "Deutsch" architecture is best known by the sturdy stone houses with adjoining barns so plentiful in the valleys east of Lancaster, Fig. 6-19. The barns themselves were imported directly from Europe. Their long roof lines and the large overhang of the second floor to provide shelter below followed the pattern set by the peasant farm groups of Upper Bavaria, where home and barn were combined into one picturesque composition. Even today the tourist who travels through this part of Pennsylvania finds evidence of foreign speech, dress, and customs all set in a simple stone and frame architecture. The drab costumes and strange traditions of these plain folks prepare one for the simplicity of their homes and for the painted geometrical symbols on their barns to ward off the evil spirits. There is a charm about these settlements which, fortunately, modern progress has not yet been able to eliminate.

Fig. 6-21. Wister's Big House, Germantown, Pa. Typical Quaker or German architecture of the early Georgian period. Doric entrance. Pent roof across end of gable.

Fig. 6-22. An example of English Georgian architecture well remembered by the builders in the late colonial period. The Old Hall, Ormsby St. Margaret, Norfolk, was built in 1735. Conspicuous details are the pedimented central bay, parapet wall with panels of balusters, brick quoins at the corners, and a belt course between floors.

AGAIN THE GEORGIAN

It was not long, however, until the popularity of Georgian arch
tecture began to assert itself with undeniable force. As the Qua¹
merchants and shipowners became more prosperous, they began
build larger and finer homes; the simplicity of the earlier houses wa
gradually replaced by the formality and pretentiousness of the Renai
sance mansions of Georgian England (Fig. 6-22). The citizens of th
middle colonies were not satisfied with the simpler forms of the
Colonial; instead the plans and arrangements of their homes rivaled
those of the mansions of Virginia in the display of monumentali·
This is best illustrated in the plan of Mount Pleasant, in Fig. 4
Most of these houses were built of masonry; some had walls of brick
laid in Flemish bond, while others were constructed of stone with
coursed ashlar, or hewn stone.

The exterior view of Mount Pleasant, shown in Fig 6-23, reveal
it as a splendid example of a monumental residence of the midd
eighteenth century. It has two flanking buildings, similar to the treatment of the manor houses of Virginia, particularly that at Mount
Airy, Figs. 8-4 and 8-6. In this Philadelphia residence, built in 1761
by John Macpherson with money made by privateering, are to
found many of the characteristics of formal Georgian architectur
Here the entrance is composed of a semicircular headed door surrounded by a Doric order of columns, entablature, and pediment, as
in Fig. 4-5. This is surmounted by a Palladian window with its three
elements consisting of the central arched opening flanked by rectangular windows. Elsewhere on the main facade there are typica
motifs inspired by Georgian houses of England: the heavy quoins
the corners of both the entrance bay and the main part of the hou
itself and the flat arches with keystones used over the windows. The
balustrades which finish the roof, together with the clustered chimneys connected with arches, help to give an additional air of pretentiousness to this mansion.

Woodford, also in Philadelphia, shown in Fig. 6-24, is another
example of the magnificent homes built during the eighteenth century
in the middle colonies. In this house, the walls are of brick and there
is a strong division between the first and second floors secured by the
use of a full entablature which continues the lines of the entablature
of the entrance.

FIG. 6-23. Mount
Pleasant, Philadel-
phia. 1761. Brick,
stone, and stucco.
Plan in Fig. 4-2.

FIG. 6-24. Wood-
ford, Philadelphia.
Eighteenth-century
brick mansion.

The development of Georgian architecture in the Philadelphia
area was encouraged by the activities of the important Carpenters
Company, an organization of architects and builders. One of their
contributions to architecture was the publication of their famous
manual with splendid plans and details. The Doric doorways at
Mount Pleasant and at Woodford came directly from the pages of
this manual. Because of the use of Georgian details of Classical derivation and the popularity of masonry construction, the formal homes
of the Philadelphia area were endowed with a heavier treatment than
that typical of the houses in the New England colonies. The columns
and entablatures used at the entrances were usually executed according to the correct proportions of Vitruvius; the main cornice of the
house generally carried modillions, or brackets, which gave a feeling
of richness and provided a repeating accent of light and shade. The
main facade was usually symmetrical in treatment. The roofs were
given importance beyond those of earlier and simpler origin. Large
urns were sometimes placed at the corners of the roof and at either
end of the ridge, as at Clivenden, or the roof was often terminated by
a balustrade as previously noted. Dormers, with scrolls at the sides
and pediments above, were conspicuous features.

As we leave the influences of the Philadelphia area, we find some
evidence of Classical correctness in the formal houses of adjacent
regions, as in Fort Johnson, Amsterdam, New York, shown in Fig.
6-26. However, the break with the stone architecture of Quaker and
German origin was usually more complete and an entirely new character was obtained. The houses were often magnificent in character,
at least in terms of the limitations and qualities of the wood with
which they were built, but their general interpretation displayed a
kinship to the homes in the New England area. This is illustrated in
the two examples shown in Figs. 6-25 and 6-29.

The Ford mansion, 1772, which is known as Washington's Headquarters at Morristown, New Jersey, has an ornate entrance executed
in the form of a Palladian motif. Here an arched opening is flanked
by Ionic pilasters supporting a richly decorated entablature. The
siding across the front of the house covers a stud frame filled with
brick and presents a smooth surface in order to simulate stone architecture; this increases the effect of monumentality—no doubt an
effort to retain the formality and grandeur of stone construction.

The general composition of Johnson Hall, at Johnstown, New

FIG. 6-25. Ford Mansion, Morristown, New Jersey. 1772. Was once Washington's headquarters. The elaborate treatment of the entrance reflects the richness of the late Georgian period.

York, is similar to the previous example. However, here the main entrance is simpler in design; it consists of a treatment composed of Doric pilasters supporting a pediment with richly accented modillions.

The interiors of the houses of the Middle Atlantic colonies, especially in the later examples, followed the general pattern set by the English Georgian and interpreted in the more pretentious homes of Massachusetts, Rhode Island, and Connecticut. If anything, the homes in Pennsylvania and New York outdid their New England cousins in their use of baroque details and achieved a richness unequaled in the houses to the northeast. Consoles and broken pediments were often used in connection with the doorways and mantels and the stairways were rich in decorative details. In plan, the houses did not vary greatly from those in New England. They were generally rectangular in shape and had the familiar central hall with its stairway at the rear or the side. In some of the more pretentious homes, notably at Clivenden and Stenton, the hall was actually a lobby or reception room with elaborate architectural features which sometimes included a fireplace.

FIG. 6-26. Fort Johnson, Amsterdam, New York. This house was built in 1749 and shows the spread of the Classical Georgian influence into the Mohawk Valley. It has a hipped roof, field-stone walls, paneled shutters, and a Doric entrance porch.

FIG. 6-27. Main entrance. Correct and beautifully executed example of the Doric order.

FIG. 6-28. Window and shutters. Here is pleasing contrast of texture and color.

FIG. 6-29. Johnson Hall, Johnstown, New York. Built in 1762. A splendid example of formal Georgian architecture with a symmetrical main facade and a hipped roof. The entrance is surmounted by a pediment. Note the early stone blockhouse-type structure at the left.

FIG. 6-30. Hall and stairway of Johnson Hall. The treatment of the stairway contrasts with that in the Hooper house shown in Figs. 4-21 and 4-22.

Chapter 7

THE ROUTE to RICHES

IN retrospect, we recall that the New England Pilgrims and Puritans produced a sturdy architecture which reflected the simplicity of their existence and the severity of their climate and that the Middle Atlantic Dutch, Quakers, and Germans developed a stone and brick architecture as evidence of their thrift and good fortune. In anticipation, we shall look to the South Atlantic colonies of Maryland, Virginia, and the Carolinas where English gentlemen and adventurers established manorial estates unique upon the American continent. Here in the South the influences of soil, climate, and people combined forces to produce homes unlike those in the more northern colonies.

COLONIZATION

As was so often the case with early attempts at colonization, much misfortune awaited the first settlers in the Tidewater region. Histories tell us that two expeditions sent by Sir Walter Raleigh made unsuccessful attempts, by probing American shores, to find gold or a route to the Orient. The first group returned discouraged to England and the second disappeared entirely, probably through massacre by the Indians.

However, the lure of possible wealth beyond the high seas was too strong a magnet to be resisted for long. In 1606 the East India Company was organized and in 1607 Jamestown was founded on the marshes of the James River. But those who invested in this company chartered by James I were impatient for a quick return on their money; they were more interested in securing wealth than in establishing communities and developing the land. This attitude naturally

116

attracted the adventurous rather than the homemaking type and, unfortunately for the success of the venture, soldiers of fortune made up the majority of the early groups. Manual labor and the hardships associated with frontier life did not appeal to these gentlemen and it was not until years later that mechanics and laborers were sent in sufficient numbers to insure successful colonization. As a result the early days at Jamestown were uncomfortable and discouraging ones and not unlike existence in the Massachusetts Bay Colony. In both the North and South, shelter was at first very primitive and the colonists were concerned chiefly with those activities related to mere physical existence.

TOBACCO

The perseverance of these English colonists in Virginia was finally rewarded. However, the wealth for which Raleigh and his followers searched was not to be found in the form of gold and spice. Gold itself was denied completely to these adventurers and withheld from their descendants for nearly two hundred years. It was not until the frontiers were pushed westward to reveal the riches of the Rockies that the dreams of the English, Dutch, and Spanish finally came true. Instead, the wealth which the settlers of the southern colonies found was a humble one. It came from the soil in the form of tobacco and rice and it helped to set the pattern of colonial life along the great rivers and the style for domestic architecture on their banks.

The colonists soon found that tobacco was a crop that required much labor in transplanting, tending, picking, curing, packing, and shipping. Since many of the early settlers came from the aristocratic class in England and did not take easily to physical labor, it was necessary to find a labor market which would supply a type of help unlike that required elsewhere on the Atlantic seaboard. It was difficult to obtain an ample supply of independent workers willing to perform the drudgery connected with the growing of tobacco; but, fortunately for the success of these attempts at colonization, indentured servants and Negro slaves became available for this work. This cheap labor was an important part of the economic life of the southern colonies and permitted the development of a single staple crop.

The establishment of the resulting large fortunes was reflected in the magnificent homes erected during the eighteenth century. The discovery of tobacco as a source of quick and steady income set the pattern for the social and economic structure of the Tidewater region. A large acreage was required for this crop, since its growth soon exhausted the soil; this created a demand for fresh land as the fields became worn out. Thus the small farm of New England had no place in the Virginia colony and the large estates of the new American aristocracy came into existence.

GENTLEMEN AND CAVALIERS

The social order of the eighteenth century in the South Atlantic colonies was a conservative one which was not affected, as was that in New England, by the industrial growth and commercial development which characterized the communities to the north. Northern trade in lumber, rum, and fish was foreign to the plantations on the southern rivers and life along these peaceful waterways developed at a more leisurely pace. The people had different objectives and methods of achieving these objectives. There was a much wider difference between the various classes of people in the Virginia communities than in the New England settlements. In Massachusetts the housewife and the hired girl were likely to come from the same social class. However, the aristocratic ladies and gentlemen of Virginia, driven out of England by the rebellion of Cromwell, were at the opposite end of the social scale from their African slaves and from even the indentured servants who performed the menial tasks of the plantation.

Thus in the Tidewater country there was fostered a feudal system of lords and serfs—a system headed by gentlemen and statesmen who did more than build manor houses as an expression of their wealth, statesmen who brought to the government of the colonies long years of experience in management. It was a stable existence which permitted and encouraged the development of important families—families whose names were significant in the social, economic, and political events of the country for many generations. As a setting for this feudal existence, large plantation homes which rivaled the manor houses of England were built along the banks of the Potomac, James, York, and Rappahannock rivers in Virginia and in the low rice lands of the Carolinas. It was truly a great period in the development of American life, culture, and architecture.

It is not surprising to find that life in Virginia was quite different from the existence of the Puritans in New England. The settlers in Massachusetts lived according to a strict moral code, which, combined with the influence of climate, developed a stern people and a simple architecture. In the South, with the freedom enjoyed within the Church of England and with the encouragement of the English court, consciences were easily placated and life was lived more fully and completely. The character and appearance of the homes of the two areas were true barometers of these differences in the two social orders.

During most of the eighteenth century there were few towns of any size in Virginia and therefore little urban social life. It was only later that the most sophisticated of the landed gentry were able to congregate during certain seasons in Baltimore and Charleston for the theater, exhibitions, and concerts. Until these mature years, the life of the South Atlantic colonies was, in general, rural in character —rural, however, in quite a different sense from that in New England. The large acreage required for the growing of tobacco necessarily meant that the plantation houses were miles apart and that each plantation was a self-sufficient community in an economic and social definition.

On these baronial estates of several thousand acres, Negro slaves and indentured white servants were organized to make each community a completely independent settlement. In addition to the slaves for the necessary housework, there were skilled craftsmen who labored as carpenters, blacksmiths, and weavers. These workmen made most of the necessities required at the manor house but many of the luxury items, such as the Georgian furniture, silverware, and costumes, were imported from England. Whereas the Pilgrims and Puritans, together with the Dutch, Quakers, and Germans, turned their backs on Europe figuratively and sometimes literally, the colonists of Virginia maintained direct contacts with business and court life in England. The absence of large towns, as centers of culture, commerce, and communication, focused attention on the fashions and gossip of London; it was to this city and the country life of which it was the center that the ladies and gentlemen of the

Tidewater region looked for their ideas of living, entertaining, and building.

The great distances that separated the various plantations and the circuitous mode of river travel necessitated by the lack of roads encouraged the development of a complete type of hospitality in each of the great manor houses. Guests came for visits, not of hours, but of days or even weeks. The plantation owners, recalling their last visit to England, entertained in a lavish manner. Horse racing, fox hunting, gambling, cock fighting, and dancing were favorite forms of diversion; the great manor houses with their dependencies were designed and furnished as a setting for this gay social life. However much these magnificent estates might have been out of place in austere New England, they were a true reflection of the domestic activities of the aristocracy of the southern colonies.

At this point it might be interesting to speculate upon the probable development of Massachusetts and Virginia if the plans of the early colonists had not miscarried in one detail. The Pilgrims were supposed to land in Virginia and it was only because of the forces of nature and the vagrancies of inefficient navigation that they found themselves ashore on the less hospitable coast of New England. We may try to imagine the kind of economic and social life these industrious but strait-laced settlers would have founded and what kind of houses they would have built in the Tidewater region. Would the Early American house have been developed in Virginia or would the influences of climate, occupation, and customs have found expression in some other form of architecture? We may ask, but our questions will remain unanswered. Of one thing we may be certain—the Georgian mansions of the great plantations would not have come into existence under dissimilar conditions.

Chapter 8

SOUTH ATLANTIC GEORGIAN

THE EARLY EXAMPLES

Before the development of the large plantation homes of the eighteenth century, the colonists of the South Atlantic area underwent privations and disappointments similar to those suffered by the settlers of New England. The groups sent out by the London Company were not chosen for their ability as pioneers and builders, and the shelters that they first erected were similar in character to those constructed in Massachusetts. The early homes were probably as poorly built of mean materials as were those of New England and naturally they have not survived the passing of the centuries. However, early in the seventeenth century kilns were built in Virginia; and domestic brick was manufactured for the more permanent homes, a few of which have been preserved until the present day.

As we have noted, the Early American house of New England exhibited a definite medieval influence in its framing, overhang of the second floor, the steepness of its roof, and the smallness of its windows. The evidence that we have of the early masonry homes in Virginia indicates a similar resemblance to an earlier period of domestic architecture. In this case, the style copied was the Jacobean, a transition in England between the Tudor Gothic and the later English Renaissance. These small houses contructed in Virginia during the last part of the seventeenth century had steep roofs, clustered chimneys, curved and stepped gable copings, mullioned and transomed windows, and other earmarks of the Tudor style. The informality of the exterior composition which often resulted from an unsymmetrical plan created a picturesque effect reminiscent of the manor houses of rural England. Bacon's Castle, illustrated in Figs. 8-1 and 8-4, displays the exterior characteristics just described. It was built in 1655 by Arthur Allen and received its name because it was seized and fortified during Bacon's Rebellion in 1676.

Many of the early homes of Virginia were simpler than Bacon's Castle in their plan and exterior treatment. In general, these early houses were one story in height, as in Fig. 8-2, and were rectangular in plan, with the main entrance located in the center of the long side. This doorway opened directly into the "hall," or living room, instead of into a small vestibule, or "porch," as in the Early American house of Massachusetts. Due to the influence of climate, the entry of the New England house was created to act as a barrier between the wintery blasts of the outdoors and the living quarters of the family; in the South, the entrance could open into the major room because the temperate weather made the vestibule unnecessary.

As we may recall, the Early American house was built around a central chimney for structural support and for the conservation of heat. In the South a type of framing different from that used in the North and the lack of a need for a central source of heat made the single large chimney unneeded and unwanted. There were, therefore, two chimneys on these early Virginia houses, one at either end of the structure. This arrangement conserved the use of brick in the end walls and also permitted the weight and buttressing effect of the chimneys to strengthen the construction of the house. These large chimneys were usually tapered in a series of steps similar to the current examples in the small Tudor or Jacobean buildings of England, as shown in the Early Colonial examples in the Glebe house, Fig. 8-2, and at Poplar Hall, Fig. 8-3.

TIDEWATER MANSIONS

With the coming of the eighteenth century, the life of the tobacco planter changed from one of limited conveniences to one of relative comfort. His holdings had been comparatively small, his servants few and poorly kept, and his house simple and unassuming. As his knowledge of agriculture grew and his profits increased, his life on the plantation became pleasant and his house larger and more nearly complete. With increased wealth and leisure time for its enjoyment,

FIG. 8-1. Bacon's Castle, Surry County, Virginia. Evidence of Jacobean influence in the clustered chimneys and stepped gables. See plan, Fig. 8-4.

FIG. 8-2. Glebe house, Charles City, Virginia. Mid eighteenth-century brick house with simple chimney and regularly spaced dormers.

FIG. 8-3. Poplar Hall, Williamsburg, Virginia. The early date, mid seventeenth century, is indicated by the tapered chimneys with paneled tops. Mansard-type roof is unique.

his thoughts turned to England with its gay social life and its magnificent Georgian homes. Under favorable economic conditions, encouraged by a mild climate and abetted by a hospitality which was to become traditional, the great period of eighteenth-century Renaissance in the South was born, grew to maturity, and flourished for many decades.

Much of the beauty and charm of the manor houses of Tidewater Virginia can be attributed to their location and setting. The Great House, as it has been fittingly called, was usually located on an elevation above the river in order that the occupants might command a view of the wharf where the ships from England docked to unload furniture, silverware, costumes, and supplies and to be loaded with tobacco and other exports. Between the house and the river was the large expanse of lawn, with its trees of cypress and oak, which gave a feeling of spaciousness and dignity to the estates, an openness which was largely missing in the homes of New England. In the rear and at the sides of the house were the flower gardens with their vine-clad summer houses and pergolas. Near the main house, and often part of a unified formal composition, were several outbuildings which housed the kitchen, laundry, dairy, and offices of the estate.

Nearby were the barns for the purebred horses and cattle, the storehouses, and the shops for the blacksmith, carpenter, and other artisans. Substantial cottages were often provided for the white indentured servants, but the Negro slaves usually lived in groups of rude cabins some distance from the remainder of the establishment. The latter arrangement is quite in contrast with the situation in New England where the hired help, recruited from a neighbor's family, was quartered in a spare bedroom under the roof of the main house or in an adjacent wing. The Virginia estate was completed by the orchards and vineyards near the house and by the many acres of tobacco land in the distance.

The early eighteenth-century houses of Virginia were smaller structures than those magnificent homes built later in the century. Usually they were rectangular buildings with plans not unlike the houses in Salem and Portsmouth. A center hall with a fine staircase was flanked by the major rooms devoted to entertainment, relaxation, and dining. The exteriors, built of brick, were two and one-half

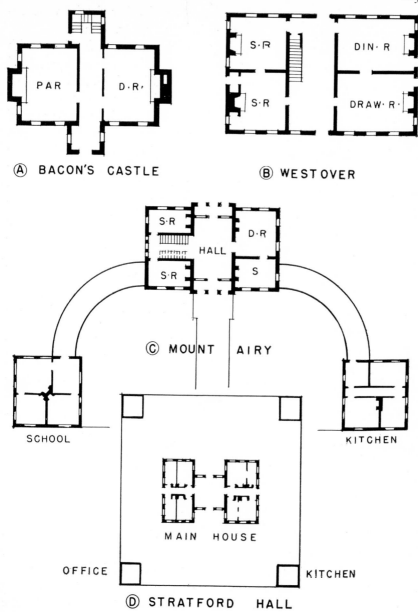

FIG. 8-4. Plans of Virginia houses, varying in size from the simple compact homes of the seventeenth century to the large eighteenth-century Georgian estates with several dependencies.

or three stories high; and the windows and other details were arranged in a symmetrical manner, as in Shirley, Fig. p-13.

However, Virginia aristocracy was not content for long with the smaller homes; instead the complete establishments represented by Mount Vernon, Mount Airy, Westover, Stratford, and others of similar character came to typify the magnificence of the Georgian movement in the Tidewater area. In these homes there was a central unit or main house with flanking or adjacent buildings or wings. The dependencies were sometimes connected directly with the house or were reached by curved or straight arcades. Often these secondary structures were completely freestanding. Whatever their plan arrangement, the manor houses were selfsufficient social and economic units and their ambitious character reflected their importance in the existence of the plantation family. They were grand in their conception, brilliant in their execution, and, even with a slight baroque note in the later examples, always in good taste. The frequent richness of Georgian ornament and the conspicuous formality of English Classicism seldom escaped the control of the gentleman designer or the professional architect.

The estate known as Mount Airy, in Richmond County, built between 1755 and 1758, burned and was restored in 1844. As will be seen in Figs. 8-4 and 8-6, it was composed of the customary central unit, with its dependencies grouped around a forecourt. A raised terrace, reached by wide steps flanked by urns monumental in scale, is a feature of the main approach. The plan of the house itself, shown in Fig. 8-4, is symmetrical in axial arrangement but not in the size of the rooms. A central hall, or reception room, extends from the front to the rear of the house, on one side of which are two major rooms and on the other two smaller rooms, once separated by a grand staircase now removed. The exterior is built of cut stone laid up in regular ashlar. Each of the two main elevations has a projecting central bay with pediment. One of these bays is treated with rusticated arches while the other has a post-and-lintel type of design. The massing of the exterior, with its hipped roof and large chimneys, gives a monumental effect reminiscent of both the English Georgian and the

Fig. 8-5 (*opposite*). Mount Airy, Warsaw, Virginia. View of garden side of house. Built in 1755-1758 this is a splendid example of Palladian-like architecture. See Fig. 8-4 for the plan.

FIG. 8-6. Entrance court, Mount Airy. Built of brown sandstone.

FIG. 8-7. View of urn in forecourt. Monumental in scale.

FIG. 8-8. Westover, Charles City County, Va. Magnificent Georgian manor house built about 1730. Steep hipped roof, tall chimneys, and ornate entrance create a feeling of grandeur and richness. Horizontal lines of the massing repeat sweep of river.

FIG. 8-9. Stairway and hall, showing paneling, mahogany balustrade, and plaster ceiling.

FIG. 8-10. Drawing room, with its large windows, paneled walls, and decorative ceiling.

FIG. 8-11. Stratford Hall, Westmoreland County, Virginia. This magnificent rural estate was built by Thomas Lee, grandfather of Robert E. Lee, about 1725. General view from the southeast, showing the main building, together with the office at the left. Plan in Fig. 8-4.

Italian Renaissance. Here are the elements of a truly magnificent baronial house and estate.

One of the most charming and beautiful of the Virginia houses is the ancestral home of the Byrd family at Westover, in Charles City County (Fig. 8-8). It was built early in the second quarter of the eighteenth century, is typically Georgian in its massing and use of details, and reflects all the wealth, polish, and social graciousness of Tidewater aristocracy. While the entire exterior treatment is symmetrical, the plan misses symmetry by reason of the off-center position of the main hallway, Fig. 8-4. The latter is located to the left of the main axis to create two major rooms on one side and two minor rooms on the other side.

The principal facade facing the James River is adorned with the central doorway which has Corinthian pilasters supporting an entablature with a scrolled and broken pediment. In spite of the baroque quality of this entrance feature, it is a fine architectural composition and one which holds its own with the many richly decorated doorways of Georgian architecture. A belt course of stone separates the first and second floors; the windows have tops of segmental arches. The main or central part of the house is two and a half stories high and is covered with a hipped roof with dormers. Four large chimneys contribute to the sense of scale and to a monumentality missing in

FIG. 8-12. View of geometrical boxwood garden, looking toward the house, gives an idea of the magnificence of the eighteenth-century Virginia estates, when tobacco left the plantation's wharf for ports across the ocean and when guests arrived for lengthy visits.

the more modest homes of New England. Low wings (formerly containing the services and now remodeled for other uses) complete the main establishment and give an interesting contrast in size and also a dignity so typical of the mansions of the period.

An estate quite unlike Mount Airy and Westover in plan and exterior treatment is Stratford Hall, in Westmoreland County (Fig. 8-4). It was built about 1725 and consists of the main house with four outbuildings or dependencies located some distance from the central unit on the four corners of a square. In these buildings were located the library, the kitchen, the school, and the office of Thomas Lee, the founder of the plantation. The entire estate is magnificently situated in the midst of broad lawns and boxwood gardens. The main house faces a beautiful vista looking toward the Potomac River. Some of these features may be seen in Figs. 8-11 and 8-12.

The house itself is *H*-shaped in plan and reminds us of the many Virginia homes with this type of room arrangement. The major rooms of the house are located on a main floor placed above a low ground floor which contained most of the bedrooms and some of the service rooms of the household. The main floor is reached by exterior stairways of stone which are monumental in character and Classical in detail, as shown in Fig. 8-13.

In the center of the symmetrical composition is the great hall, or

Fig. 8-13. Stratford Hall. Detail of southeast entrance, showing one of the monumental exterior stairways with Classical balusters. Flemish bond design shown in the brickwork of the first floor. Clustered chimneys with connecting arches are unusual.

salon, square in shape, which provides access to transverse halls between the four rooms in each leg of the *H*. The great hall is one of the largest and most magnificent early paneled rooms in the South Atlantic colonies. Its main wall divisions are marked by Corinthian pilasters supported by pedestals between which are panels with delicate moldings. These panels concealed the books which were carried to the adjacent library for use by the early occupants of the house. A complete entablature carries around the room and receives a break above each pilaster, and there is a decorative candelabra in keeping with the character of the room.

The two wings of the *H* were originally divided into eight nearly equal rooms, four in each leg of the composition. However, near the beginning of the nineteenth century considerable remodeling took place; some of the partitions were moved and the character of the interior trim was changed. In each of these eight rooms, now unequal in size, is a large fireplace which is unique with Stratford Hall. The openings of these fireplaces are spanned by segmental arches and the surrounding plastered surfaces in the originals were

FIG. 8-14. Fireplace in kitchen. Segmental arches of this type, with simple mantels, were used in the fireplaces of main house. Kitchen faces office across court.

without the usual paneling and mantels, similar to the kitchen fireplace, shown in Fig. 8-14, the opening of which is twelve feet long and seven feet high.

The exterior walls of Stratford Hall are built of brick laid in Flemish bond, that is, with headers or ends alternating with the side faces of the bricks. The brick used in the walls of the ground floor are larger than usual and differ both in color and size from the smaller pink brick in the walls above the projecting water table. The windows in the ground floor walls have segmental arches while those of the main floor are treated with flat arches of brick set on end. In addition, the entrances are built of brick with projecting cornices and pediments of the same material. This uniform use of a single material gives a simplicity of treatment which is lacking in most of the later examples. The fine grouped chimneys, with their Flemish bond details, molded projections, and semicircular connecting arches, are unique features and present a composition unlike most of the Georgian work in this country.

All the homes built in Virginia during the eighteenth century

Fig. 8-15. Exterior view, Roper house, Williamsburg, Virginia. One of earliest houses in town.

Fig. 8-16. Window detail, Roper house. Original walnut sash, shutters, and pulleys still in use.

were not as magnificent as Mount Vernon, Mount Airy, or Stratford Hall. Instead many beautiful and interesting frame houses, such as those at Williamsburg, Figs. 8-15 and 8-17, were constructed on the smaller estates and in the settled communities which began to appear as the region became more thickly populated. In some respects these more modest houses, with their walls of white clapboards, their regularly spaced dormers, and their red brick chimneys, bear a resemblance to the homes of New England. However, the similarity is only a superficial one because the informal spirit is quite unlike that of the houses of Massachusetts or Connecticut. The Georgian ancestry, common to both, is present in these picturesque structures of old Virginia but the large chimneys betray their southern origin.

OUTSIDE VIRGINIA

While the individual plantations of the South Atlantic colonies were little villages in themselves, the feudal system which made them possible could not hold out indefinitely against the economic

FIG. 8-17. St. George Tucker house, Williamsburg, Va. Built about 1789. Unsymmetrical massing, simple cornice, dormers, and large tapered chimney are typical of period.

FIG. 8-18. Brafferton Hall, president's home at William and Mary College, Williamsburg, was built in 1732. The brick walls were laid up with alternating headers and stretchers to form a Flemish bond pattern. The hipped roof and heavy chimneys give an air of dignity.

need for the development of urban communities. As a result of increasingly steady pressure, occasioned by the industrial and commercial expansion in the North and the growing population in the South, the cities of Baltimore, Annapolis, and Charleston became centers of population and produced a distinctive type of domestic architecture.

One of the investors in the Virginia Company, who combined adventure in the Virginia colony with a gamble on the uncertainty of colonization, was Lord Baltimore. He secured a grant from Charles I and founded the colony of Maryland. He made special inducements to gentlemen of means and less attractive offers to those who could only till the soil. The economic experiment was a successful one and Maryland became another land of large estates but one which also had a sprinkling of small farms held by middle-class farmers. The city of Baltimore, the origin of whose name is obvious, was founded early in the eighteenth century. Here and in the neighboring town of Annapolis are to be found even today a number of interesting houses of a type quite unlike those built as the center of plantation life.

The Paca house and the Brice house, Figs. 8-19 and 8-20, located in Annapolis, show the influence of the restrictions of urban life. The plantation type, with its wide spreading lawns and separate dependencies, is missing in these examples. The Brice house has low wings on either side but, in general, these town houses were compact structures somewhat similar to the larger homes in Salem and Portsmouth. The wings of the Brice house, hidden by the foliage in Fig. 8-20 but similar in scale to the dependencies of the Paca house, emphasize the large size of the central unit. Still further emphasis is given by the steep roof and the tall end chimneys, all resulting in a monumentality comparable with the dignity of the contemporary English Georgian. This house and others in the area had a simplicity, however, which distinguished them from the manor houses of England or even from those of the colony to the south. The entrances were relatively simple in design and the treatment of the windows and cornice correspondingly unpretentious. The Brice house was built in 1740 before the Renaissance influence became pronounced. In the Paca house we find that the informal massing, steep roof, high chimneys, and unadorned brick walls repeat the spirit of the best architecture of early Maryland.

Fig. 8-19. Paca house, Annapolis, Maryland. From photograph before 1890.

Fig. 8-20. Brice house, Annapolis. Built 1740. Typical of period.

The plague and the great fire of London depleted the fortunes of Charles II and those of his court; as a result several of the friends of the English monarch, who were to be called Lord Proprietors, received in 1663 grants of land in the region south of Virginia. Thus Charles Town, as it was called until 1783, was founded in 1670 on a peninsula between the Ashley and Cooper rivers which converge to form a magnificent harbor. The presence of this harbor contributed in no small way to the development of the city and to the erection of the many fine homes. While the name of the town indicates its English origin, its population was a mixture of Dutch, Irish, and Quakers, together with the English and the French Protestants who arrived in 1680.

The social lines of Virginia and the caste system of England prevailed in Charleston and its environs. The early Cavaliers and the owners of large estates dominated the social and economic life until the merchant princes emerged from the class of early traders and shopkeepers. The harbor was always filled with ships and the wharves were stacked high with indigo, lumber, rice, and corn. The wealthy merchants were quite able to build magnificent brick houses which they furnished with fine Georgian furniture brought over from England. Charleston was thus the center of gay entertainment —festivities encouraged by the presence of the ships in the harbor and the influx of visitors from the adjoining plantations. Here was bred the hospitality which later spread westward and became so characteristic of the homes of the Deep South. Charleston was not a rough, uncouth city, but, instead, was a progressive and cultured community with newspapers, concerts, libraries, schools, and theaters. This advanced social order was expressed in the fine homes which even today greet the tourists in this romantic old town of the Colonial South.

After the establishment of Charleston, many settlements made their appearance up the several waterways of the colony. Life along these rivers was very much as it was in Virginia. The rich soil of fine loam encouraged the planting of a number of crops, but rice became the economic backbone of the colony. Rice did for Carolina what tobacco had done for Virginia and what cotton was to do later for

FIG. 8-21 (*opposite*). Thomas Heyward house, Charleston, South Carolina. Built in 1750, it once had a two-story veranda. Compare with the later houses in Salem, Figs. 12-3, 12-5, 12-7. Washington stayed here in 1791.

the Gulf states. The city of Charleston owed much of its history, wealth, and architecture to the influences of the plantation country. The planters combined with the local merchant princes to dominate trade, politics, and culture. The families of these planters built magnificent summer homes in Charleston and fled to them in the summer to escape the mosquitoes and the fever of the swamps. Here they remained until the killing frosts of autumn made their plantation homes safe for their return.

Early in the eighteenth century a law was passed in Charleston requiring all houses to be built of brick. This desire for permanency accounts for the popularity of brick houses, a popularity that outlasted the law which was eventually repealed because of the scarcity and cost of brick. In spite of the fact that many of the fine homes still standing in Charleston belong to the Post-Colonial and Greek Revival periods, the eighteenth century is well represented by a number of houses which reflect the influence of the Georgian.

One of these is the Heyward-Washington house (Fig. 8-21). Here is a three-story house with brick walls and a symmetrical treatment of the main facade. The center doorway, with its engaged columns, arched opening with paneled jambs, and simple pediment, is a conspicuous and decorative feature of the exterior composition. The interior of the major rooms and the fireplace treatment are typically Georgian in the character of the various architectural motifs. Here is the familiar mantel and overmantel with ears and the beautifully paneled doors which are to be found in the Colonial examples of all the English colonies.

Another of the eighteenth-century houses is to be seen in Fig. 8-22. This is the Izard house, which was built about the middle of the century. While the arrangement of the fenestration is generally symmetrical, the entrance is located in an off-center position and thus plays a minor part in the composition. With the stucco finish applied to the brick walls and with the wrought-iron balcony under the central second-floor pair of French doors, the house reveals the possible influence of Mediterranean architecture.

The house which was originally owned by Miles Brewton and is sometimes called the Bull-Pringle house, shown in Fig. 8-23, was

Fig. 8-22 (opposite). Izard house, Charleston, South Carolina. Exterior walls of brick and stucco. Built before 1757. The windows and balcony give evidence of Mediterranean influence.

F IG. 8-23. Miles Brewton house, Charleston, South Carolina. Built in 1765.
Two-story porch with stone columns. Drawing room across front on top
floor. Occupied by British during Revolution.

built in 1765. In many respects it is unlike other homes of the period
and, on the other hand, like many of the later houses which showed
the Classical influence. Its double portico, with Doric columns on
the first floor and Ionic on the second, is similar in general appearance to the two-story porches which were added to Shirley, Fig. p-13,
some years after this Virginia house was built. With this the similarity ceases to be pronounced; the Miles Brewton house has a hipped
roof instead of the mansard type, the scale is smaller, and the character
is simpler than at Shirley.

Chapter 9

THE SPANISH CONQUESTS

We have become so accustomed to thinking of the American colonies in terms of those located along the Atlantic seaboard, all of which were settled largely by the English, that we are inclined to forget the many attempts of the Spanish and the French to establish new empires on this continent. It is true that the English were destined to rule much of seventeenth- and eighteenth-century North America and that the English tongue, rather than the Spanish or French, was to become the language of most of that region. However, there were times when the economic and architectural history of Europe and America depended upon the victories of an army or navy; the Treaty of Utrecht in 1713 and the Treaty of Paris in 1763 marked the end of wars, the transfer of territory, and the shift of architectural influences. There were crucial days on this continent, as well as abroad, when the chateaux of France and the castles of Spain might have crowded out the manor houses of England; it is only by a combination of circumstances that our home life, customs, traditions, and domestic architecture are predominantly English in character.

INVASION

During much of the sixteenth and seventeenth centuries the Spanish Empire was the strongest political and military power in the world. The force which expelled the Moors from Spain, turned back the Turks sweeping over the Mediterranean countries, and held at bay the armed might of France and England was the same force

143

which carried on the conquest of Central and South America. Operating from bases in the Caribbean, the Spanish gained a foothold in Florida and attempted to establish settlements along the South Atlantic and Gulf coastlines. Missions were built in Georgia and North Carolina; and, as the early English settlers were gaining an insecure foothold in Virginia, the Spanish adventurers were casting covetous eyes toward the entire Tidewater area.

But English influence soon became strong and the English outposts along the valleys of the Cumberland and Tennessee rivers secured the southern region against permanent settlement by the Spanish traders and missionaries. Thus only a few buildings remain in Florida as a reminder of the ambitions of the Spanish early in the eighteenth century. One of these is the Fatio house, St. Augustine, shown in Fig. 9-1. In this example the stucco walls, projecting second-floor balcony, and tile roof repeat the semitropical architecture of the West Indies and the minor buildings of mother Spain.

In the southwest, the story was the same as in Florida except that the setting and the time were different. It is true that Spanish armed might and Castilian culture left a wider and more vigorous mark upon the great Southwest than in the Gulf area, but it is also true that the Spaniards finally lost their hold upon this part of the American continent. First the Spanish governors were pushed out of Mexico; Mexico, in turn, through political and military reverses, was compelled to relinquish to the United States the land north of the Rio Grande. By the middle of the nineteenth century, the area from California to Texas came under the control of an English-speaking country and the direct influence of Spanish culture and architecture came to an end. Thus significant economic and political events shape the character of the architecture which shelters our domestic activities; victorious armies and navies dictate the style of our homes.

But before the Spanish lost their New World colonies, they had dominated the arid areas of the great Southwest for nearly two centuries. The culture which had been established in Mexico for many decades spread northward beyond the Rio Grande. Early in the eighteenth century, the priests, soldiers, adventurers, and settlers who pushed into the present states of California, Arizona, New Mexico, and Texas discovered a docile Indian civilization which accepted their domination and a native adobe architecture which needed only further development. The Spanish conquerors found pueblos

FIG. 9-1. Fatio house, St. Augustine, Florida. Evidence of early occupation of South-eastern United States by the Spanish. Balcony and tile roof show Mediterranean influence.

built of sun-dried brick, rough stone, and adobe. These houses had flat roofs carried on wooden beams which projected beyond the face of the walls, a feature shown in El Palacio Real de Santa Fe, Fig. 9-2. Since there was a scarcity of other materials, the Spanish were compelled to build in the manner of the Indians, modifying their construction and design only enough to permit the erection of buildings for their special ecclesiastical and secular needs.

SPANISH BUILDINGS

The most ambitious buildings of the Spanish colonial period were the missions, which were located at strategic points, often a day's journey apart, along the California coast and inland to the east as far as San Antonio. The padres and their Indian servants built informal and picturesque structures of stone, adobe, timber, and tile. Usually the various units were grouped around a large open court surrounded with cloisters, their tile roofs contrasting pleasantly with the plastered walls. From the original Indian pueblos and the smaller and more intimate portions of the missions came the inspiration for the detached houses which were to be built in the Southwest during the eighteenth and nineteenth centuries.

Most of the houses exhibiting Spanish influence which are still standing in the states along the Rio Grande were constructed in the early part of the nineteenth century. Often these structures were built around two or three sides of a courtyard, or patio, which provided the outdoor living quarters of the family. The interior court of the mission was the center of many of the activities of this ecclesiastical-secular organization and, in a like manner, the patio with its fountains, trees, shrubs, and flowers was the scene of the family life of the early ranchero. The corridor, or porch, with wooden posts or brick piers supporting a simple shed roof of colorful tiles was a conspicuous feature of these homes, as shown in the Vhay house, Santa Barbara, Fig. 9-6. The rooms generally opened directly upon this porch and provided the usual facilities for living, dining, sleeping, and for the services. In some instances there was space for a family chapel and a guest room.

The walls of these houses were usually made of sun-dried brick covered with plaster and whitewashed. Because of the scarcity of timber, little wood was used except for the windows, doors, and roof timbers. Windows were barred with grilles of wood or iron in accordance with the practice in Spain and in most instances were not glazed. The only fireplace was in the kitchen, and no heat was provided elsewhere in the house during the winter months, resulting, no doubt, in rather cheerless interiors for a portion of the year.

The interiors of these Spanish houses were generally as simple as the exteriors. The walls were plastered and whitewashed but the monotony was sometimes relieved by accents of brilliant color in the painted wooden doors, the tile floors, and occasionally in the plain, sturdy furniture. Usually the furnishings corresponded to the character of the house itself. In the more modest homes, a few chairs, benches, tables, and beds constituted the sole furnishings; but in the larger haciendas the appointments were as fine as those in Spain. Here the floors were covered with carpets, and windows were decorated with brocaded curtains. Sofas and chairs were upholstered in velvet, while the chests and tables were often reinforced with wrought iron and decorated with Moorish details.

Fig. 9-2. El Palacio Real de Santa Fe, New Mexico. Adobe-type walls. 1609.

Fig. 9-3. Kit Carson house, Taos, New Mexico. Mid nineteenth century.

Fig. 9-4. Mazieres house and store, San Antonio, Texas. Built 1854.

FIG. 9-5. Caretaker's house, Ranchos de Taos, New Mexico. Early nineteenth century. Here is a typical house of adobe construction, with projecting ends of timber roof beams. The informal massing is characteristic of Indian architecture of the Southwest.

FIG. 9-6. Vhay house, Santa Barbara, California. Built in 1825 by Indian laborers directed by Franciscan friars. The roof tiles were made at a nearby mission.

Chapter 10

THE ADVENTUROUS FRENCH

EARLY COLONIZATION

The French Empire in America, at its greatest period of strength during the seventeenth and eighteenth centuries, was a rival of the English colonies, a rivalry which lasted until the period immediately preceding the Revolutionary War. But the French offered serious threat to English supremacy only in isolated instances, for the colonists of New France were outnumbered by those of New England by a ratio of one to ten. In spite of the attempts by the French—the efforts of Jacques Cartier and Samuel de Champlain, the activities of the French missionaries and trappers, and the presence of settlements at Detroit, Mackinac, Green Bay, St. Joseph, and at the confluence of the Mississippi and Missouri rivers—early French colonization was not successful except in the lower St. Lawrence Valley.

Much of the ill luck of the traders and adventurers who penetrated the Great Lakes area was due to the lack of assistance from the French government; consequently permanent and prosperous communities did not develop and the homes which were erected in most areas were usually of a temporary nature. The more ambitious houses built in the Quebec area resembled those of Burgundy with their thick walls of gray stone, hipped roofs, and round towers, but this style did not spread into the settlements to the South and West. Perhaps this was due in part to the constant conflicts between the French and the English which extended from the St. Lawrence down the Mississippi to the Gulf of Mexico. War followed war until the peace of 1763 which signalized the supremacy of English traditions and architecture.

THE PERMANENT RECORD

In Louisiana the French were more successful in leaving evidence of their architectural heritage than they were in the area of the Great Lakes. By canoe and flatboat on the Mississippi and by sailing vessels directly from France, the French colonists converged on Nouvelle Orleans near the mouth of the great river, a city founded by Bienville early in the eighteenth century. New Orleans remained a French city until the transfer of Louisiana from France to Spain in 1762 when, with its cosmopolitan population, it was forced to adapt itself to Hispanic influence.

Two fires during the last few years of the eighteenth century wiped out most of the earlier French buildings and those which today attract the tourists to Vieux Carré, or the Old Square, date from the early part of the nineteenth century. They are the product of the Creole culture of the period, which was a mixture of French and Spanish influences flavored with a dash of American seasoning. One of these picturesque buildings is shown in Fig. 10-1. This is the Mayor Girod house which exhibits the specific details and general character so peculiar to the buildings in the towns of France. The wide entrance doorway with its segmental arch and the French doors opening onto balconies with graceful wrought-iron railings reveal the origin of the exterior treatment.

Today on Rue Royale and adjacent streets are to be found many old buildings identified with the lives of Jean and Pierre Lafitte, Lafayette, Andrew Jackson, and other romantic and important persons. Here memories of the past still cling in spite of the commercialized sight-seeing tours of the present day. Here, side by side, are structures which remind us of the Renaissance architecture of old Spain and those which take us back to the villages of France. Through the many arched entrances we may catch glimpses of paved courtyards with their balconies, galleries, fountains with tropical plants and flowers, and slave quarters. Behind the shuttered windows life still goes on at a leisurely pace, unspoiled by the traffic of a modern city a few squares away. Here a different climate and people combined to create a culture and a domestic architecture in this part of colonial America quite unlike those which developed under the influences of the stern attitudes of the Pilgrims and the severe winters of New England.

FIG. 10-1. Mayor Girod house, New Orleans. French influence.

FIG. 10-2. Spanish Custom house, New Orleans. Plantation type. 1784.

From a humble collection of huts and cabins, New Orleans was destined to grow into the capital of New France in the South. It merged the nationalities of many countries and was, in turn, a French, Spanish, and antebellum southern city. It prospered as the sugar and indigo plantations were developed along the banks of the Mississippi and as the city became a great seaport for the export of the products of the Middle West. It became the center of the immense financial, social, and political life of the lower Mississippi Valley, an area in which magnificent homes were to be built by a later generation.

While the Colonial plantation homes, bowing as they did to the will of climate, were to influence the form and character of those which followed a few decades later, they were quite unlike the representatives of the Greek Revival or even their contemporaries in New Orleans constructed on crowded city streets. These homes of the early planters were squarish structures with wide verandas on all sides of the house. Heavy Doric columns were usually used on the first floor, with a modified form on the second. Large French casement windows opened onto the galleries, all a concession to the hot, humid climate of the region. A curving hipped roof accented with dormers was a conspicuous feature of the exterior composition. These characteristics are shown in the old Spanish Customhouse, Fig. 10-2. No doubt houses of this type can trace their ancestry to the West Indies, where the influences of weather and customs were not dissimilar to those of Louisiana.

But the Colonial architecture of the delta was destined to come to a rather abrupt end, as the French and Spanish movements, like the Hispanic in the Southwest, were curtailed by political developments abroad. Napoleon, having forced from Spain the cession of Louisiana, weary of war and afraid of the maritime power of England, sold to the United States in 1803 the great French empire west of the Mississippi. Thus French colonization was at an end and French architecture, except for that imported by later revivals, ceased to exert much influence upon the domestic buildings of this country.

Part TWO
THE NEW REPUBLIC
THE POST-COLONIAL PERIOD

Chapter 11

THE NEW ERA

PATRIOTISM AND PROSPERITY

THE American Revolution witnessed the end of the great period of colonization and the beginning of the era of expansion. The multitudes who came to the shores of this country after the War of Independence gave impetus to the growth of the eastern seaboard and to the westward movement of the American frontier. By this time, the English had established themselves firmly in the New England colonies and in the Tidewater area of the South Atlantic region. The Swedes, Dutch, Quakers, and Germans had settled in the middle colonies and some had moved west and south in search of cheaper land. The French had come down the Mississippi and left their relatively unimportant mark upon the architecture of the delta country. The Spanish had penetrated the Southwest and developed an architecture indigenous to the arid country adjacent to the Rio Grande. The forces which were to mold modern America and the homes of America were already at work, forces which were constantly being modified by ever changing social, economic, and geographical conditions and by recurring penetrations from abroad.

It must be remembered that the War of Independence was inspired and carried on by an energetic and determined minority. The people of New England and Virginia supported the struggle with enthusiasm but many of those in Pennsylvania, New York, and New Jersey were apathetic or even hostile to the armies of Washington. Allegiance to the British crown was discarded slowly and often reluctantly and, in many areas, the break with England was not a sudden or complete one. The conflict had been not so much a war

against the mother country as a war to perpetuate the liberties up
which the colonies were founded.

With the successful completion of the war, there was, therefor,
less anti-British feeling than might be expected against a formei
military and political enemy. This was reflected in the architectur(
and furnishings of buildings belonging to the decades immediately
following the Revolutionary War. The people who lived along the
Atlantic seaboard continued to look to England for inspiration and
guidance in the design of their homes until other influences came to
these shores by way of changing social and political conditions.

It is not to be inferred that life in the colonies continued to follow
the pattern of colonial days, for, in spite of the absence of a complete
break with England, the struggle for freedom brought a number of
changes which were to affect the growth of cities and the construction of homes. Since this country no longer belonged to the British
Empire, American ships could not compete on an equal basis for the
trade of English colonies. They were forced to seek new ports of
call. This turned out to be a blessing rather than a calamity. China
was the terminus of new trade routes and, with the development of
the speedy clipper ship, the merchant fleets of the new republic begar
to dominate the seas. In this they were aided by the strife and in
security which Napoleon created with his ambitious military cam-
paigns; for several decades the ships carrying the Stars and Stripes
returned to the seaport towns of Boston, Salem, Portsmouth, New
York, and Charleston laden with goods from all parts of the world.
This brought prosperity to these and smaller communities and permitted the construction of the magnificent homes which are to be
found still standing today along the elm-lined streets of some of thes
cities and towns.

Chapter 12

THE GEORGIAN CLIMAX

ARCHITECTS AND WOOD CARVERS

SINCE the American Revolution brought political liberty without artistic and cultural freedom, the years following the war saw the development of a pro-English type of Renaissance architecture which we now call the Federal or Post-Colonial style, or, for this discussion, the Georgian Climax.

The wealth of the shipowners and merchants of the coastal cities encouraged a rich type of domestic architecture which formerly had been confined almost entirely to the plantation homes of the Tidewater country. Now, as the designers of houses grew more skillful and came less under the influence of academic Classicism, the exterior treatment and interior adornment of homes took on a new and more ornate character. As the result of adherence to English tradition and style, the American architects of the period became familiar with the works of an English architect–cabinet maker by the name of Robert Adam. Adam had been inspired by the monuments of imperial Rome. At first he had interpreted the details of his buildings in a strictly classical manner; but, as he continued commissions for his friends and other important people of London, he imposed his own personality upon the designs in the form of attenuated proportions and delicacy of treatment. With this basic foundation of Classicism, modified by the style of Louis XVI, the Adam style became popular in England at the time that America was ripe for a movement away from the academic Georgian (Fig. 12-1).

In bringing this new style to this country and in directing its development for the treatment of Post-Colonial homes, individual architects played a more important part and received greater recogni-

FIG. 12-1. Home house, Portman Square, London. 1775-1777. View of music room. A splendid example of the work of Robert Adam at the height of his career. The lavishly decorated interior, with pilasters, swags, and ornate plaster ceiling, is refined and delicate in character. Compare with interior, Cook-Oliver house, Fig. 12-4.

tion for their design ability and leadership than was the case during the Colonial period. From abroad came such important figures as Benjamin Henry Latrobe, James Hoban, and others, to be joined in the practice of architecture by such men as Samuel McIntire, Charles Bulfinch, and John McComb. The various handbooks of the Colonial period were still used as sources of inspiration but the designers of the Georgian Climax era drew more and more upon their own inventive ability.

The Georgian Climax in domestic architecture covered a span of years from about 1790 to 1820. The style was still based on the Georgian Colonial, and at times it was difficult to distinguish one from the other. This Post-Colonial architecture found its more fertile field for development along the New England coast, as the well-to-do shipowners and merchants used their newly acquired wealth to build magnificent homes in the seaport towns. Thus in Boston, Providence, Salem, Newburyport, and Wiscasset the lighter and more graceful

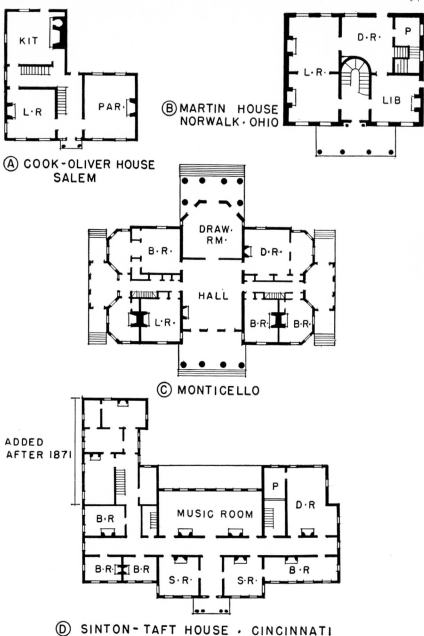

Ⓐ COOK-OLIVER HOUSE
SALEM

Ⓑ MARTIN HOUSE
NORWALK·OHIO

Ⓒ MONTICELLO

Ⓓ SINTON-TAFT HOUSE · CINCINNATI

FIG. 12-2. Plans of representative houses built during the decades immediately following the Colonial period. Many plan arrangements of the Post-Colonial style were complex in character.

expressions of Georgian architecture appeared. In addition, as men of wealth and culture moved westward through the valleys of the Mohawk and the Ohio, even to the rolling lands of central Kentucky, the style spread to many other parts of eastern United States.

THE POST-COLONIAL HOUSE

In the numerous examples of the period, and especially as the style moved westward away from the source of inspiration, there seemed to be less and less adherence to Georgian proportions and details. In many of the buildings there was a conscious striving for a greater richness in effect but this was accompanied by a pronounced delicacy of treatment. The moldings were generally smaller and the columns more slender and attenuated. While the scale of the various elements grew smaller, the size of the major parts of the building became larger. Ceiling heights were increased, windows and their glass divisions were made bigger. The steeply pitched roof of the Colonial style was replaced by a hipped roof of low pitch or by a flat roof hidden behind a balustrade. Thus the roof became a relatively unimportant feature of the exterior composition of the Post-Colonial house. In New England the houses were built of brick or of wood either frankly used or often designed to simulate masonry construction with flush siding and imitation stone quoins at the corners. Throughout the back country and west to Kentucky, brick was a popular building material during this period.

The traditional Colonial plan was abandoned for one which permitted greater freedom in planning. Whereas the plan of a pre-Revolutionary house in New England had usually consisted of a square or rectangular area with four rooms and a central hall and stairway, the plans of the later Georgian houses consisted of numerous rooms, closets, and hallways. The major rooms and lobbies were often elliptical or circular and there was a variety of gracefully curved stairways. On the interior, the color of the Colonial was replaced by a treatment calling for a somewhat monotonous use of white. The walls usually consisted of painted plaster above a simple wainscot. The cornices of the rooms, the entablatures of the doorways, and the carving of the pilasters and the capitals were composed of delicate moldings and decorated with graceful swags, garlands, and urns.

Throughout there was a feeling of elegance which helped to create a correct setting for the beautiful mahogany furniture of Hepplewhite and Sheraton design and for the brocades, silver, glass, and porcelains which were brought from foreign countries. But the fragility of the beauty shortened the life of the style. The first few years of the nineteenth century were still in the age of the frontier. This was a time when the wilderness was conquered only by the immense drive and vitality of the American people. The style was, therefore, too ethereal to hold its own against the demands of a rugged frontier life and, in spite of some acceptance beyond the Alleghenies, it was doomed to be replaced by the robustness of the Classical movement.

SAMUEL McINTIRE

One of the most prolific and talented of American designers, who assisted in transplanting the Adam style from England to this country, was Samuel McIntire. He began as a wood carver and later became widely known as the architect who helped to transform Salem and Portsmouth from Colonial towns into representative cities of the new republic. Thus he belonged to that group of men who changed the architectural face of New England after the American Revolution. He designed many of those magnificent homes which were monuments in themselves and which also influenced the appearance of simpler homes along the paths of emigration to the West. His houses followed the same pattern of development taken by the work of his master, Robert Adam, in England. At first his houses were heavy and monumental with a definite feeling of academic correctness. In his later examples, there is evidence of the gracefulness and refinement that characterized the more attenuated phases of the Adam style.

The houses of McIntire were usually rectilinear in mass and dignified in character. They were three stories high, especially those in the cities, and were surmounted by a hipped roof. This treatment permitted the cornice to be carried around the four sides of the house and give emphasis to the horizontal line of this decorative element.

Fig. 12-3. Cook-Oliver house, Salem, Massachusetts. Built in 1802 by Samuel McIntire. Typical stately three-story frame house of the Post-Colonial period.

FIG. 12-4. Cook-Oliver house, Salem. Doorway in first-floor hall, as remodeled in 1808. Delicate Adamesque treatment. See plan of house in Fig. 12-2.

Fig. 12-5. Loring-Emmerton house, Salem, Massachusetts. Mansion type.

Fig. 12-6. South entrance, with Ionic porch and Palladian window.

FIG. 12-7. Phillips
house, Salem, Mas-
sachusetts. Note
quoins at corners.

FIG. 12-8. Detail of
entrance, with fan-
light and side lights.

The exterior treatment usually fell into a stylized pattern; the fenestration was more or less uniform in spacing and departed little, except in detail, from the preceding Colonial arrangement. There were generally five bays, or openings, across the main facade, with the Classical orders used chiefly at the entrance. However, there were exceptions to this arrangement in which large fluted pilasters framed the corners of the building and extended from the ground level to the heavy crowning entablature, as in the Peirce-Nichols house in Salem. In the early examples the simple Doric order was used to create a square or semicircular portico for the entrance, the Doric losing favor in the later years to the more graceful Ionic. As the Adam influence gained ascendancy over the earlier academic treatment, the doorway became enriched and enlarged by the inclusion of the fanlight above the door and by the side lights on the sides.

Above the entrance and lighting the second-floor hall was the familiar Palladian window, Fig. 12-6, consisting of an arched opening flanked by rectangular openings which extended to the spring line of the central arch. This window was the object of much thought and decoration. The entire motif, often set within a larger recessed arched opening, made use of small columns, pilasters, and entablatures, combined with keystones and other decorative devices. The balustrade around the deck of the roof, an element present in many of the finest houses of the Colonial period, was continued as a feature of the exterior composition.

The so-called Cook-Oliver house, Fig. 12-3, was built for Samuel Cook in 1802, after designs by Samuel McIntire. The sketches that McIntire left show a center-hall type of plan symmetrically arranged, with a kitchen ell added to the rear on the left-hand side. The very fine gateposts and fence are also included in the drawings signed by McIntire and are similar in general character to others in the old town of Salem. The doorway in the first-floor stair hall, Fig. 12-4, gives some indication of the lateness of the work and its similarity to the Adam style in England (Fig. 12-1). The delicacy of the carving and the small scale of the various parts create a feeling of refinement which reveal the Post-Colonial ancestry of the house.

The Loring-Emmerton house, in Salem, shown in Fig. 12-5, and the Phillips house, Fig. 12-7, nearby, are splendid illustrations of the formality and richness of the Post-Colonial period. They make use

FIG. 12-9. Phillips house. View of fence with decorative posts using the Doric Order.

FIG. 12-10. Loring-Emmerton house. Side fence. Posts with delicate moldings and details.

FIGS. 12-11 and 12-12. Details of tops of fence posts in front of Phillips *(left)* and Loring-Emmerton *(right)* houses. In one example, the conventionalized urn is a conspicuous decorative element; in the other, the ball crowns an Ionic treatment with a pilaster and voluted capital.

FIG. 12-13. Peirce-Perry house, Newburyport, Massachusetts. Built in 1810.

FIG. 12-14. Fence patterns also used in roof balustrade. Narrow siding.

Fig. 12-15. 1801 House, Belfast, Maine. Federal-type house with flat roof, balustrade, and cupola. Entrance porch with Greek Doric columns, forerunner of the later Classical treatment.

of the same exterior composition as that in the Cook-Oliver house and repeat in their entrances and gate posts the sophistication of the Adam style.

Fig. 12-16. House built in Columbia Falls, Maine, 1818, for a lumber baron, Thomas Ruggles. Front wall is of wood chaneled to imitate stone. Main cornice and cornice of porch are composed of delicate open details quite unlike the plain moldings of the Georgian, but reminiscent of the Adam style.

THE INFLUENCE SPREADS

While these beautiful and stately houses were being built in Salem, others of similar character were appearing elsewhere along the Atlantic seaboard and as far west as the Ohio Valley area. The John Brown house, Providence, Fig. 12-17, is similar in its general composition and fenestration to the Loring-Emmerton house in Salem. In the Brown house we find the usual projecting entrance porch above which is a richly decorated Palladian window. A pediment at the top of the central bay interrupts a graceful balustrade of turned spindles.

Down east on the rocky coast of Maine almost to the New Brunswick line, the graceful Adam-like style early in the nineteenth century penetrated deep into the wilderness. At Columbia Falls the Ruggles house was built as architectural evidence of what money and a cultivated taste could create in a raw country far removed from the cultural centers of Massachusetts. The simple, dignified house with its delicate and refined details (see Fig. 12-16) was de-

FIG. 12-17. John Brown house, Providence, Rhode Island. Late eighteenth-century mansion. Entrance porch with Palladian window above. Conspicuous balustrade on roof.

FIG. 12-18. Martin house, Norwalk, Ohio. A simple and modified version of the Post-Colonial style. Composition different from New England examples: two stories instead of three; wide porch instead of smaller entrance; stepped gable instead of hipped roof. See plan, Fig. 12-2.

FIG. 12-19. Blacklock house, Charleston, South Carolina. 1795. Low ground floor.

FIG. 12-20. Graceful Adamesque entrance, with exterior stairway.

FIG. 12-21. Liberty Hall, Frankfort, Kentucky. Built in 1796. Brick walls.

FIG. 12-22. Graceful Doric entrance with Palladian window.

FIG. 12-23. Rose Hill, Lexington, Kentucky. 1820. Resembles Homewood.

FIG. 12-24. Looking from drawing room into dining room.

signed by Aaron Sherman, a carpenter-architect from Duxbury, Massachusetts.

Farther to the south, in Charleston, was a different but equally handsome version of the late Georgian style. This is illustrated in the William Blacklock house, Fig. 12-19, which was built in the late eighteenth century. Here is the same dignity and monumentality, the same use of brick walls, ornate entrance, and symmetrical fenestration as we find in houses farther north. However, there is one difference. The humid climate of South Carolina has caused the development of an unimportant ground floor and the creation of an important first floor for the major rooms high above the damp ground.

Conspicuous architectural details are the semicircular blank arches above the first-floor windows, Fig. 12-20; the unique triple window on the second floor, and the segmental arch for the fanlight in the pediment at the top of the central bay. Attention may be called to the beauty and delicacy of the treatment of the main entrance, where the tracery of the leaded glass and the accents in the entablature contrast pleasantly in color, scale, and texture with the surrounding brickwork. Buildings of this type and quality add immeasurably to the charm of Charleston, just as their cousins in time and character help create the beauty of Salem.

The Martin house at Norwalk, Ohio, Fig. 12-18, is an entirely different version of the Federal, Post-Colonial, or late Georgian, period, the choice of name depending on the personal attitude of the observer. Here is another brick house with an entrance porch that is three bays wide and makes use of the Ionic order. The two-story walls are terminated by an entablature and balustrade of wood across the front and by stepped gables and high chimneys at the ends. While the porch is comparatively light in character, the house itself has a heavy simplicity which betrays its distance from the New England sources of inspiration.

Only two decades after the signing of the Declaration of Independence, Liberty Hall was built in Frankfort, Kentucky. Daniel Boone had scarcely pushed his way through the mountains from North Carolina and the village of Frankfort had a population of only six hundred persons. It is, therefore, surprising to find here in the wilderness a substantial brick mansion as beautiful and sophisticated

Fig. 12-25. Taft house, Cincinnati, Ohio. Built about 1820 and attributed to Benjamin Latrobe as the architect. Similar in general composition to Homewood. Plan is shown in Fig. 12-2.

as the one shown in Fig. 12-21. While the details were interpreted somewhat differently from those belonging to the homes in New England, nevertheless the same arched entrance flanked by fluted Doric columns and surmounted by a Palladian window is a conspicuous feature of the front facade. Here is a slightly different quality, an individuality which is understandable in light of the possible influences of a new country, but basically this house is a close kin to those near the Atlantic Ocean.

In the interior of this house is the familiar center hall with its broad stairs down which have descended generations of blushing brides or charming hostesses to greet friends and relatives below. On one side of the hall is the parlor and the dining room while on the other side is the drawing room and the first-floor chamber. Across part of the second floor is an area which was formerly the ballroom but which was later remodeled into a chamber and library. Thus we see that the people of the pioneer movement were not entirely without the usual social amenities and cultural attainments. This house remained in the Brown family from the time it was built in 1796 until a few years ago, which accounts for its fine state of preservation and for the original furniture, silver, and china which it contains.

Before we leave the Georgian Climax, it seems proper to present two houses which are similar to each other but in many respects quite

F IG. 12-26. Homewood, Baltimore, Maryland. Built in 1807 in the manner of Robert Adam. Intimate in scale and size, in contrast with the large manor houses of Virginia. See detail in Fig. 12-27.

unlike the homes created by McIntire in the north or those by Thomas Jefferson in the south. In time of construction and use of Classical details these houses have much in common with the architecture of these two master architects but, in the final analysis, their treatment is as different as day is from night.

In spite of the fact that the architectural procession in the South Atlantic states seemed to by-pass the slender Adamesque version of the Renaissance, there is one important example of this style in the estate of Homewood, near Baltimore. Its southern ancestry is betrayed by the higher central unit flanked on the sides by lower wings for the services, as shown in Fig. 12-26. Throughout the entire composition there is a feeling of grace and delicacy which compares favorably with the work of McIntire in New England. The slender Corinthianesque columns of the entrance portico, the tall windows with shutters, the restrained cornice, and the low hipped roof all combine to create an architectural composition quite in contrast to the Palladian Doric of Jefferson's Classical houses in Virginia to the south. Homewood was built shortly after 1800, in that transitional period between the decline of the Georgian and the rise of the Classical.

The same general composition and character displayed in the design of Homewood are repeated in the Baum, Sinton, or Taft house (to give its various names) in Cincinnati, Fig. 12-25. This house was

Fig. 12-27. Entrance portico of Homewood. The Adamesque delicacy of treatment is apparent in the capitals, cornice, and pediment. Compare with the heavy treatment of the entrance at Monticello shown in Fig. 13-2.

built in 1820 by Milton Baum and has been attributed to Benjamin Henry Latrobe. It has the same pedimented portico with four columns, even though the latter are coupled instead of being spaced more nearly equally as at Homewood. The walls of this house are covered with flush boards to give the impression of the use of stone but this attempt to imitate masonry construction did not prevent the designer from achieving a lightness and delicacy typical of the Adamesque movement. In plan, Fig. 12-2, the central unit of this house has two sitting rooms across the front, flanking the entrance hall, while at the rear is a larger and more majestic music or ball room, together with several smaller rooms. Naturally the house, like most houses which have survived generations of use, has been remodeled to meet changing needs. Originally the plan approximated a simple rectangle, but after 1871 the bedroom wing was added to the left rear. The music room was created in 1895 by combining three smaller rooms, while in 1900 the dining room was enlarged to its present size.

FIG. 12-28. Home of John Henry, father of Patrick Henry, near Charlottesville, Va. Built in the eighteenth century, later moved, enlarged, and restored. It is now known as the Michie Tavern. The composition of the main mass is similar to that of the Skinner house.

FIG. 12-29. Skinner house, Hertford vicinity, North Carolina. Built about 1800. The tall tapered chimneys recall the treatment at Tuckahoe, Va. Note two-story porch.

Chapter 13

THE INFLUENCES OF ROME

TO EUROPE AGAIN

IT was not until the second decade of the nineteenth century that the new republic was willing or able to forsake the leadership of England in matters cultural and architectural. The bitterness engendered by the War of Independence was just wearing off when the forces which brought about the War of 1812 came into being. Because of this later alienation and because of events that took place outside the British Empire, America definitely turned away from Georgian England for architectural inspiration. In her role as a new and ambitious country, the United States sought and received recognition in the capitals of Europe.

France, who had been our ally against England, emerged from the confusion of the postrevolutionary period as the country that was closest to us spiritually, culturally, and politically. Furthermore, we were bound to France by the common experience of purge by revolution. These social and intellectual ties with a free France, coupled with the advances made by science in most of Europe, set in motion in this country forces which were to culminate in the Industrial Revolution in our economic life and in the Classical Revival in our architectural development.

Perhaps the action of turning to the Classical for inspiration was not so much a matter of ignoring established English traditions as it was the following of thought and action typical of most of western Europe. The writers who molded the thinking of both England and France, sensing the superficialities of the Renaissance, decided to go directly to the underlying source for the basis of their philosophy. The Renaissance had been built upon the foundations of the Classical and it was, therefore, logical to return to fundamental truths for aid in material and spiritual progress. Under astute leadership, it became popular for people to be interested in Greek and Roman mythology, and the Classical Revival was born in Europe.

When the style was transplanted to America, it found the citizens of the new republic ready for a new movement and its acceptance was thus an eager and enthusiastic one. The life and ideals of the Roman republic had no difficulty in capturing the imagination of those who were building the American republic from the ashes of an English colony. Roman architecture seemed to symbolize the dignity and power of this young country; and, after its trial for public buildings, it set the style for several decades of domestic structures.

WASHINGTON

The architecture of the South Atlantic states missed much of the transitional movement separating the Georgian style from the Greek Revival. Except for a few examples, the Post-Colonial Adamesque movement did not gain much of a foothold in the Tidewater area, and thus there fell upon the shoulders of Roman architecture the task of bridging the gap between the eighteenth-century Colonial and the later movements. This role was well carried by a few men in the buildings which they designed and built. Great manor houses were constructed in Virginia during these decades but they were cast in a form and decorated in a manner different from that employed by the earlier designers. This allegiance to the Classical spirit was due to two influences—one, a great city, Washington; the other, a great man, Thomas Jefferson.

The daring appeal of the monumental layout of Washington, created by the French planner Major L'Enfant, made an impression on the American people when they were forsaking English in favor of continental ideals and encouraged them to turn their backs even more completely upon their former sources of inspiration. Thus the Roman Classical, borrowed from Paris, which had been transformed from a medieval town into a monumental city, set the style for the design of the new capital of America and, later, for the homes of America.

FIG. 13-1. Monti-
cello, Virginia. East
front. Designed by
Thomas Jefferson.
1770-1809. Plan in
Fig. 12-2.

FIG. 13-2. East por-
tico, showing Roman
Doric treatment.

FIG. 13-3. Bremo,
Fluvanna County,
Virginia. South
front. Formal plan
with dependencies.

FIG. 13-4. Entrance
portico. Note simi-
larity to Monticello.

Fɪɢ. 13-5. Battersea, Dinwiddie County, Virginia. Built in 1765, altered in 1800. Attributed to Jefferson. Central block, with stair hall and salon beyond. Palladian-type Roman country house. Red brick walls now covered with stucco.

THE GENIUS OF JEFFERSON

Collaborating in guiding the design of this new capital city were the two great political leaders of the time, George Washington and Thomas Jefferson. Each of these gentlemen had more than an amateur's knowledge of architecture and each had the vision and enthusiasm necessary to found the city and to insure its development as a monument to American patriotism and power. Washington built Mount Vernon as a great manor house in the Post-Colonial manner but it is to Thomas Jefferson that we turn as the great architectural leader of the Classical movement. In many respects Jefferson was the Leonardo da Vinci of the new republic. He wrote the Declaration of Independence, was Governor of Virginia, and President of the United States. He designed public and domestic buildings for the rolling hills of Virginia and invented furniture and equipment for his own comfort and for that of his friends. He was a statesman and scientist, an artist and engineer. He was an ardent believer in democracy and he, more than any other, turned for his architectural inspiration away from the aristocratic richness of Georgian England to the democratic simplicity of Classical Rome.

Fig. 13-6. Belle Grove, Middleton vicinity, Virginia. A Classical Revival house built in the late eighteenth century. Stone walls with quoins at corners. Wide entrance porch with Doric columns. Note hipped roof and tall chimneys.

This fondness for Classical architecture was not accidental. After the American Revolution, Jefferson traveled extensively in western Europe. In Paris he saw the glories of Rome transplanted from the Pantheon to the Invalides and the Louvre. He admired the Maison Carrée in Nîmes and compared its monumentality with the delicacy of the Georgian and Adamesque designs of earlier decades. He believed that the scale and dignity of the Roman temple were more symbolic of American drive and energy than was the intimacy of the Colonial; when he returned to this country, he found its people receptive to the architecture of Rome.

In spite of Jefferson's enthusiasm for Classical forms and details, he did not reproduce them in his domestic architecture with archeological exactness. He was always conscious of the influences of local materials, climate, and craftsmen. Even his own favorite treatment, the Roman Doric, was applied to buildings whose plans and exterior massing were far different from temple architecture. The columns, entablatures, balustrades, and doorways were correct enough in their details and proportions but they were combined with brick walls to create a composition which had a distinctive American flavor. As a further difference: while the architecture of Thomas

183

Jefferson was a monumental one, it also had a reserve which was in keeping with the modesty of the man, a simplicity in contrast with the more ornate buildings of imperial Rome. There are not many structures that can be directly attributed to Jefferson but he had a profound influence upon his contemporaries; his buildings, while important in themselves, also helped to pave the way for the acceptance and growth of the Greek Revival style which was to follow.

The earliest house designed by Jefferson and the one for which he is best known is his own home at Monticello. He worked on it for many years, from 1770 on, but most actively from about 1796 to 1809, creating the designs, making the drawings, and superintending the construction. The structure, as it was finally built after many studies, is in plan a symmetrical composition with a projecting central salon, flanked by two other important rooms terminated by polygonal bays at the ends (see Fig. 12-2C). The exterior treatment is large in scale and all considerations are subordinated to monumentality. The central feature of each major facade is a correctly proportioned Palladian portico using the Roman Doric order. From one view, a balustrade all but hides the low pitched roof; while from another view a low dome, set upon an octagonal drum, rises above the balustrade and dominates the composition. In the interior, the rooms have high ceilings with complete entablatures of Classical elements and proportions. The doorways are composed of molded jambs surmounted by pediments designed in the true Classical manner. Throughout the building there is a feeling of heaviness in contrast with the delicate refinement of the Colonial and Post-Colonial styles.

The house at Monticello was laid out as part of a large plantation, as drawings by Jefferson indicate. He intended that a great forecourt with offices and other buildings joined by an architectural treatment should assist in creating a manor house in the Palladian Roman style rivaling the finest of the homes of the earlier Georgian period. The view, shown in Fig. 13-1, gives some indication of the magnificence of the house itself; however, it does not show the rooms for the services which are such conspicuous features of the groups at Stratford Hall, Mount Airy, and Bremo. At Monticello, Jefferson subordinated the dependencies to the main house by concealing them beneath the long terrace extending from the house on either side. Under the south terrace were the kitchen, smoke room, and dairy—

a group which terminated in a small pavilion above grade. This pavilion was the first building erected on the site and it was to this modest home that Jefferson brought his bride in 1772. Under the north terrace were housed the stables, carriage house, and laundry; thus a general plan similar to that at Bremo was created. In the latter building, however, the architectural treatment is more monumental and conspicuous than at Monticello, as shown in Fig. 13-3.

Another outstanding example of the Roman Revival style is the house at Bremo, which, as has been indicated, is similar in character to Monticello. Bremo was built in 1818 by John H. Cooke and, if Jefferson was not the actual designer, the house at least reflects his influence. As will be seen in Fig. 13-3, the building consists of the customary center unit with flanking wings, all connected by covered corridors. The view shown is the garden side of the house, which has as its axial feature the arched loggia on the ground floor, above which is the recessed bay with columns.

The entrance motif, shown in Fig. 13-4, is similar to that used at nearby Monticello, Farmington, and Estouteville in that it employs the same Roman Doric columns with a pediment. This entrance is on the opposite side of the house from the garden view shown in Fig. 13-3.

The ground floor of the main house contains the dining room, library, pantry, and storerooms, while the major living rooms and chambers are on the upper floor. In the wings are housed such facilities as the kitchen, laundry, servants' rooms, harness room, and schoolroom. The wings are more monumental in treatment than is usually the case with the dependencies of these southern homes. At Bremo the end of each unit is terminated with a two-story porch composed of an arcade on the first floor which supports a heavy order with pediment on the second level. This adds to the dignity and formality of the entire composition.

Altogether Bremo more than holds its own among the great manor houses of Virginia, whether they be of Georgian or Roman derivation. Here Classical symmetry and grandeur assert themselves quietly but emphatically for the delight of those who may journey to the vicinity of Charlottesville and neighboring communities.

Chapter 14

THE CHANGE IN CHARACTER

THE period of architectural development in America which we call the Greek Revival lasted from shortly after the War of 1812 until just before the Civil War five decades later. Even though it was confined to the first half of the nineteenth century, it is a part of our history that, in contrast with colonial times, belongs to present-day America.

The years before the Revolution are in the dim and distant past. In the minds of recent generations, the colonial period was more closely related to Georgian England than to early America. While many examples of Colonial architecture have survived, the habits, dress, utensils, and equipment of those days are associated with people with whom we have only a reading acquaintance. The three-cornered cocked hats, the embroidered coats, the sack-backed dresses with stomachers, and the wigs and queues now seem to belong in museum cases rather than upon ladies and gentlemen. The great differences between our prosaic twentieth-century conveniences and the more romantic but less efficient eighteenth-century methods of working, cooking, and lighting seem to separate us entirely from colonial days.

THE SPIRIT OF THE TIMES

In contrast, the turn of the nineteenth century actually marked the beginning of our present-day culture and way of life. Many con-temporary things and practices were conceived during the Greek

Revival period. Until this time, man had made progress slowly in the development of the techniques of working and living. Horse-drawn vehicles had carried the followers of Julius Caesar, William the Conqueror, and Charles I. The good citizens of Boston rode uncomfortably in stage coaches to Salem or Providence. For centuries, homes had been heated by fireplaces and illuminated by candles. The land had been tilled with the crudest of tools and the crops harvested by methods hundreds of years old. Cloth had been woven on hand looms and metals had been forged on the anvil.

But the Greek Revival period witnessed the early years of the industrial age. During the first half of the nineteenth century, steamboats and passenger trains began to replace the sailing vessels and the stage coaches. Cast-iron stoves became a greater convenience than fireplaces and oil lamps took the place of candles. The iron plow and the mechanical reaper removed some of the drudgery from farm work; cotton and woolen mills replaced home industry; rolling mills, rather than hand forges, converted iron into tools and utensils.

These years during the first half of the nineteenth century were vital and dynamic ones in the development of America and its domestic architecture. Since 1776 the American people had been busy establishing their newly gained independence on a firm basis; while a new nation was being born geographically and politically, a new nation was also being born industrially and architecturally. But even with this growth, it was, nevertheless, a period of mixed blessings; some of the changes were for the good, some were of questionable merit. Undoubtedly America gained in material progress. Labor-saving machines made it unnecessary for families to be self-sufficient units. People no longer had to make their own furniture, clothing, and equipment. Some of the drudgery was taken out of work activities—family life and domestic architecture felt the impact of this change.

However, America lost in spiritual progress. The beginning of the machine age spelled the doom of the beautiful craftsmanship of colonial days. The graceful and delicate details of Hepplewhite, Chippendale, and Sheraton were replaced by the uniformity of machine-made furniture. In architecture, the richness of the hand-carved Georgian gave way to the straight lines of the Greek style and later to the confusion of jig-saw ornament.

By now our break with England was complete; two wars in little more than a quarter of a century had created an irritation that even the ties of a common language, commercial contacts, and family connections could not overcome. By now there was wealth in this country and, therefore, added time for leisure, contemplation, and education. Industry, trade, and agriculture collaborated in the development of a prosperous nation in which the simple magnificence of the Greek Revival style found a ready acceptance. America was beginning to be conscious of its need for a new culture; it became popular to have a knowledge of the civilizations of Rome and Greece. Georgian architecture was completely in the past; now we turned even from the Roman architecture of Thomas Jefferson to that which came from Athens.

The popularity of the movement was due, in part, to the interest which this country displayed in the Greek war for independence against the Turks. America had just gone through a struggle for freedom; it naturally looked toward a similar contest in far-off Greece and its sympathy went out to these valiant people. Thus wherever new towns were built, along the paths of immigration during the early half of the nineteenth century, this sympathy was reflected in the names given to these communities. Consequently the names and architectural forms of Greece are scattered across the eastern half of the United States in Ithaca, Ypsilanti, Troy, Athens, Euclid, Delta, and Sparta. Here and elsewhere, Doric, Ionic, and Corinthian temple forms are reflected in the buildings of the Greek Revival.

A POPULAR ACCEPTANCE

In New England the Colonial tradition held until well into the nineteenth century, especially in the older communities. This is understandable when we remember that the eighteenth-century Georgian style was so satisfactory in its application to homes that it has persisted for two hundred years. It is little wonder that its popularity would not yield easily to the first new architectural movement that challenged its position. The Greek Revival style is, therefore, more conspicuous in the younger towns or in those that developed during the second quarter of the nineteenth century. Even though it was surrounded by the Colonial, the new Classicism was well received in various parts of New England. Thus many towns up and down the coast from Connecticut, through Rhode Island and Massachusetts, to Maine are as Greek in their architectural character as others are Colonial. It is possible, therefore, to place these communities in the stream of history by a study of the style of their homes. New Haven, Providence, New Bedford, Nantucket, and Worcester have many fine examples featuring the use of Greek columns and entablatures. Belfast, Ellsworth, Bangor, and Calais in Maine are as Classical as Wiscasset is Post-Colonial.

It happened that the opening of the area west of the Alleghenies coincided in time with the introduction of the Greek Revival style into this country. It is therefore understandable that many houses with Grecian details are to be found along the routes of travel which led into the new lands of the Middle West and the South. In the North, people from New England followed the valley of the Mohawk and the Erie Canal westward across New York and spread out through the Finger Lakes district. Here, at Geneva, Utica, Syracuse, and Canandaigua, the triumph of the Greek Revival was complete.

Under the influence of relative peace and prosperity that followed the Revolutionary War and the War of 1812, the attention of the American people was directed toward the improvement of travel and transportation. Highways were built to connect the cities along the coast and also to reach into the backwoods country. Many turnpike companies came into existence; the roads that they constructed, together with the canals, held supreme as a system of transportation until supplanted by the railroads. The Cumberland Road, or the National Pike, was completed to the Ohio River in 1818 and in 1825 its extension through Ohio, Indiana, and Illinois was authorized by Congress. Along this turnpike, Fig. 14-1, poured the emigrant families and their household goods in the popular vehicles of the West, the Conestoga wagons. These wagons, with their red and blue bodies and their coverings of white canvas, carried the national colors into the new country while their owners carried the spirit of Greek architecture into the settlements along this arterial highway.

FIG. 14-1. Old toll house at "Jug" Bridge, near Frederick, Maryland, on the Old National Trail, which helped to carry the Greek Revival style into the Ohio Valley.

THE OHIO RIVER

Generally paralleling the old National Pike was the traffic on the Ohio River. The early raft held more household goods than did the wagon and, except for occasional catastrophies, river travel was easier and faster. As the century progressed, flatboats and keelboats were added to the river traffic and, by the middle of the century, steamboats had generally replaced the earlier types. It is not difficult to understand why the Ohio River held an important place in the settling of the Middle West. Its location and direction made it the broad highway of early nineteenth-century commerce. Its easy current flowed to the West and was an open invitation for a comfortable ride to the lands and riches beyond the eastern settlements. It tapped a country abounding in natural resources and thus tied the agricultural West to the industrial East. It carried settlers onward to new opportunities and later brought their produce back to established markets. Along the Ohio are now to be found countless examples of the movements in domestic architecture that occurred after the Colonial period. Those who peopled and developed this rich and

Fig. 14-2. Jacob Conser house, Jefferson, Oregon. This house with its slender Doric columns indicates the spread of a modified Greek Revival treatment as far west as the Pacific coast. It was built in 1854 by the owner of one of the first saw mills in Oregon.

fertile region during the nineteenth century wrote a veritable history of, first, Greek and then, later, Gothic and Victorian homes.

Thus the Ohio River became the crossroads of America and Cincinnati was known as the Queen City of the West. The westward march of the Greek Revival style through Ohio began at Marietta and extended across the state, influencing the building of Zanesville, Chillicothe, Norwalk, Columbus, Dayton, Cincinnati, and many other communities. This part of the old Northwest Territory was originally penetrated a few decades previously by pioneers who, because of their precarious economic status, built only the simplest kind of shelter. Hence the Greek Revival style came into a raw and undeveloped country and was used for homes both modest and magnificent. Scattered along the early highways to the West, there are, even today, many simple and unpretentious houses whose antecedents can be traced, by the presence of a plain lintel over the window or a pilaster at the side of the door, to more ambitious neighbors farther up the road.

After establishing itself in the Ohio Valley, the Greek Revival

style continued to follow the paths of the restless pioneers as the
spread out in search of new opportunities until even the Far We
felt the influence of this movement. In such towns as Ann Arbo
(Michigan) Madison (Indiana) and Ottawa (Illinois), to mention
just a few on this side of the Mississippi, are to be found splendid
examples of Greek architecture used in the treatment of early nineteenth-century homes. Across the prairie states and the Rocky
Mountains, the style maintained its popularity; it traveled with the
early settlers to California and Oregon and was responsible for the
design of the house shown in Fig. 14-2.

THE PIONEER

While frontiersmen and pioneers were largely instrumental in
increasing the size of eighteenth-century America, these later hardy
settlers were even more active in the nineteenth century during the
spread of the Greek Revival movement. Stately houses with Greek
columns appeared in the wilderness almost before the region was
cleared of the Indians, because of the indomitable spirit of the
earlier pioneers.

As these intrepid settlers pushed into the Middle West, the new and
often inhospitable environment helped to mold a new breed of men
and women. These people were more independent of eastern influences and leaned less upon European customs and traditions. They
developed their own methods of building homes and making furnishings. The ability to read was now much more common than during
the early days of the colonies; the increased number of books and
magazines from England found a wider circulation and brought a
flood of ideas and information about matters architectural and other-
wise. But in spite of these contacts with Europe, the home-builders
and homemakers of the Middle West had progressed far enough in
time and distance from the domination of foreign influence to insure
an American flavor to their lives and their belongings.

Here we should pay tribute to the role of the American woman in
the development of society from its frontier pattern to its more refined manifestations. When the family moved from the relative comfort and safety of the settled areas to the less secure surroundings of
the West, many new and arduous tasks awaited them. It was the

man's job to clear the land, build the house, and make the living. He
was a rugged individual, who, in order to hold his own in the rough
life of the frontier, had to give his attention to the material things
of life.

His wife had the even more difficult task of adapting herself to
the hardships of a primitive existence. But in spite of the demands of
frontier activities, and in spite of the fact that she worked in the
fields, wove cloth, processed food, and carried the full burden of
household duties, she also tried to keep alive a spark of the more
pleasant life which she had led in the East. It was she, rather than
her husband, who maintained, even in the wilderness, the traditions of
family life. She made a home from a house, giving it those qualities
which were then almost entirely feminine. She hung the curtains and
grew the flowers. She created the demand for new furniture which
was either made by the craftsmen of the family or brought overland
from eastern cities. While the husband was tilling the soil or trading
for profit, the wife was maintaining the desirable social amenities.
She nurtured the culture of the nineteenth century and brought it
to fruition in the house of her choice. She demanded the changes
that brought wood instead of dirt floors, window glass instead of oiled
paper, and chairs in place of stools. Later she insisted on upholstered
furniture of fine woods which, in turn, called for plastered walls,
interior paneling, and rich accessories. She gave dinner parties, provided music, and encouraged polite conversation. The frontier was
conquered by the courage and strength of the man; the frontier was
made acceptable and the home attractive by the wisdom of the
woman.

THE DEEP SOUTH

While the North and West were being settled and homes were
being built in the Greek Revival manner, a similar development was
taking place in the Deep South. The area along the Gulf had not
figured prominently in the colonization of the eighteenth century.
For the most part, it was isolated from the trade routes of earlier
generations and its development was retarded until the early nineteenth century. The South had long been an inhospitable area. In
the early days, Spain held the seaports, while strong Indian tribes

controlled the interior. But settlement was inevitable. In the Gulf states, backwoodsmen moved along the streams, clearing the land and establishing communities. These pioneers were followed by the planters with their slaves who founded the cotton plantations and built the Greek Revival homes.

During the first half of the nineteenth century, life in the Deep South became stabilized at a leisurely pace. The long coastline and sheltered waterways provided an easy system of transportation. The warm climate and slave labor combined to slow the tempo of living; and, in this backwater of semi-isolation, the South did not get into the swift Northern current of competition for railroads, labor, and markets. The immigrants from Ireland, Scandinavia, and Germany were not attracted by the slave economy of the South but chose, instead, the industrial opportunities of the North. The South, in general, remained a homogeneous region in population and architecture—a region with an intellectual and economic self-sufficiency and one which took to its bosom the stately and dignified style of the Greek Revival. The plantation home with its tall columns and deep porches thus became a perfect setting for the tranquil family life of the period.

With the invention of the cotton gin and the establishment of cotton as a staple crop, this part of the country was ripe for nineteenth-century growth and for a favorable reception of a new architecture. Thus we find today in the cities of Richmond, Charleston, Athens, Nashville, Mobile, and New Orleans and on the countless plantations along the southern rivers many splendid versions of formal homes with Greek columns, pilasters, and entablatures.

However, there was one fundamental difference between the acceptance and the use of the Greek Revival style in the South and in the North. This difference grew quite naturally and directly from the variations in the social classes of the two parts of the country. In the North there were many small merchants, artisans, and professional people who comprised a large middle class. The Greek style was used in the design of shops, churches, and homes for these people —used in a way that was democratic and widespread.

By contrast, the South was a land of extremes in wealth and culture; at one end was the plantation owner and his family, at the other end were the plantation workers. The middle class, so necessary for a well-rounded culture and architecture, was largely missing in this social order based on the economy of slave labor. The great variety of buildings necessary to house the activities of the middle class was likewise missing in the southern states. Therefore the important buildings, executed in the style of the Greek Revival, were the great plantation homes; the more modest structures comprising the towns along the Ohio River did not appear in the settlements along the lower Mississippi.

GREEK PATTERNS

Impetus was given to the growth of the Greek Revival style by the discovery of the Elgin marbles, a collection of Greek sculpture from the Parthenon, and by their appearance in London. The interest which these events aroused in England in Greek architecture was transmitted to this country and aided in popularizing the movement in America. Thus the Greek Revival was simply part of a wider movement, but it was far enough removed from the influences of Europe to have a distinctive American flavor.

While the details of the Greek style (Fig. 14-3) were interpreted differently in various parts of the country, as climate and economic conditions affected the development of the style, the use of books of both English and American origin helped to exert a unifying influence. As was the case with Colonial architecture, there were many books published to guide the designers of Greek Revival homes. Perhaps the most important was one entitled *Antiquities of Athens* by Stuart and Revett which was printed in England late in the eighteenth century. In addition, *The Practice of Architecture* by Asher Benjamin and *The Beauties of Modern Architecture* by Minard Lafever, the latter published in 1835, were two popular American books that described the details of the Greek style. Again the conditions of the Colonial period were repeated by the scarcity of practicing architects. Generally the client simply showed selected pages from the handbooks to the builder and asked him to produce a house with the desired characteristics.

In addition to the regional variations, the style was further divided according to the degree of adherence to Classical proportions and to the academic use of details. In many homes of both the North and

Fig. 14-3. Temple of Nike Apteros, 438 B.C. A small temple in the group on the Acropolis, displaying the Ionic order with the familiar volutes in the capitals. This type of treatment served as the inspiration for the Wilson house, Fig. 15-1.

the South, porticoes of Greek Doric, Ionic, and Corinthian design formed the major portion of the front facade. Often these Greek elements were copied with extreme fidelity and retained much of the character of the buildings of antiquity. The moldings around the doors and windows repeated those found on Greek temples and it was only in the massing of the building and the disposition of the openings that the designers departed from the Greek pattern. In other examples there is definite evidence that the ingenuity of American craftsmen and the independence of American designers resulted in a pronounced break with tradition. Often the columns of the portico or porch were square instead of round, and at times the portico was replaced by a pedimented end of the house with flat or paneled pilasters instead of columns. In addition, the massing of some houses departed from the temple form and became quite informal and unsymmetrical in treatment and composition.

In spite of its many variations and its freshness, the Greek Revival was, in general, a sentimental style which was reflected in varying degrees in the literature, art, costumes, and manners of the people. It was an artificial, though popular, movement and one which was largely unrelated to family life. For the most part, it produced a style of architecture in which internal planning was subordinate to exterior proportions and treatment. It flourished for nearly half a century, flourished at a time when the prosperity of the country could give to the style the elegance with which it was rightfully endowed.

However, the very prosperity that encouraged its development helped to spell its doom. The *nouveaux riches* were not content for long with the simplicity of the Greek style as evidence of their social and economic importance. The good taste that was characteristic of the domestic architecture of the first half of the nineteenth century gave way to the confusion of the baroque, or rococo; and several eras of bad taste followed in rapid succession. The style passed also because it was a derivative architecture and therefore lacked the stability of a really indigenous movement. The very process of copying and adapting led to a habit of borrowing from Europe which could not be broken. The opiate soothed and lulled. The designer could not resist the drug; more and more it became fashionable to turn to England for the Gothic, to Paris for the Renaissance, and to Provence for the Romanesque. But while the Greek Revival lasted in this country, it was magnificent!

Chapter 15

YANKEE AND ANTE-BELLUM MANSIONS

IN THE NORTH

THE Greek Revival treatment was used for all types of dwellings, from town houses with narrow facades facing the street to freestanding homes of different sizes and shapes. The plans varied from symmetrical versions of the Colonial type with a central hall combined with parlors, reception rooms, and dining rooms to the many examples of unsymmetrical arrangements. When the symmetrical plan was abandoned, the resulting patterns were quite varied in character and details. The style never attained the informality of the Gothic, but considerable freedom in planning was achieved within the restrictions of the style. *T*- and *L*-shaped structures were quite common, sometimes with the rooms of the main unit composed formally, sometimes with the entrance and hallway at one corner of the main facade. The latter arrangement was often used in connection with a symmetrical portico. Variety was a conspicuous characteristic of Greek Revival buildings; it is difficult to point out a single building as one typical of the movement.

One of the most characteristic of the symmetrical types is based on the form of the Greek temple. It is possible that the templelike exterior was first used for public buildings where the accompanying dignity and monumentality had a universal appeal. In the temple type (Wilson house, Fig. 15-1) the narrow end of the house was turned to the street in contrast with the Colonial practice of having the long side parallel to the street. The ridge of the roof was carried

FIG. 15-1 *(opposite)*. Judge Wilson house, Ann Arbor, Michigan. A graceful and stately entrance portico with fluted Ionic columns. The walls are of brick covered with stucco. Built about 1836. Plan in Fig. 15-7.

forward to form the apex of the pediment, which, with the remainder
of the entablature, was carried on Doric, Ionic, or Corinthian columns. When the long side of the house was turned to become the
main facade, the pediment was usually abandoned in favor of a flat
entablature carried by eight columns. The portico of the narrow
type house, which extended across the front end, and at times across
the rear end, usually had an even number of columns, four or six in
number, and an odd number of bays, or spaces between columns, in
order that the center bay was in line with the entrance on axis, as
in Fig. 15-7. This count did not always hold, however, because the
entrance was sometimes not on center, and this arrangement often
encouraged the use of an even number of bays. In some of the less
pretentious homes, the portico was eliminated entirely in favor of an
end wall decorated with a simple pediment and pilasters. This is true
of those houses whose narrow gabled ends faced the street and usually of those with unsymmetrical arrangements of doors and windows.

Regardless of whether the temple form was retained unmodified
or was combined with flanking wings at a lower height, the familiar
Greek details were unmistakably conspicuous. Everywhere there was
evidence of the heavy simplicity of the Greek style. Typical Greek
moldings were used around the doors and windows, as illustrated in
Fig. 15-2. The anthemion or honeysuckle ornament and the antefixa
ornament were employed as decorative accents in the more pretentious exteriors and interiors, while in the frieze of the entablature
were to be found the Greek fret and the pierced grille, as in the
Anderson house, Fig. 15-3. The pilasters at the corners of the house
and those used around the doorway were sometimes paneled instead
of unadorned. The doorway, in either the symmetrical or unsymmetrical facade, was likely to be composed of plain moldings or a
heavy order of columns or pilasters supporting a simple entablature,
as in Fig. 15-6. The materials used in the wall construction of Greek
Revival homes were brick or wood, with indigenous stone employed
in occasional examples.

In the interior of these houses, one finds today the same spirit of
Greek simplicity that was employed on the exterior. Often the scale

Fig. 15-2 (*opposite*). Wilson house, Ann Arbor. Interior view of a parlor
window. The verticality of the window repeats the proportions of the exterior
portico. Example of Classical simplicity.

Fig. 15-3. Anderson house, Ann Arbor, Mich. Temple-type Greek Revival house built in 1836. Entrance portico has heavy Doric piers supporting a modified entablature with pediment. In the architrave and frieze are grilles of Greek design and small windows.

Fig. 15-4. Campbell house, Mt. Carmel vicinity, Ohio. Built in 1804 of pine trees cut in North Carolina and floated to the site. Porch with Doric columns and piers.

Fig. 15-5. Hurst house, Dover, Ohio. For plan see Fig. 15-7.

Fig. 15-6. Greek influence shown in pilasters and simple moldings.

of the rooms and of the decorative elements was monumental in character. The fireplace, together with the moldings used at the doors and windows, was composed of familiar Greek details which harmonized with the dignity displayed elsewhere in the building.

In a random selection from the countless splendid examples of Greek architecture, the Wilson house at Ann Arbor, Michigan, Fig. 15-1, is first presented for analysis. This house has a two-story portico with fluted Ionic columns and an authentic entablature and pediment. This composition is extremely graceful and dignified and repeats many of the qualities of the best of the Greek work. The view of one of the windows, Fig. 15-2, shows the consistency which existed between the character of the exterior and the interior. With the plainness and simplicity of the pilasters and entablature surrounding the window, the verticality of the composition is in keeping with the proportions of the entrance portico.

Another house in Ann Arbor is the Anderson house, shown in Fig. 15-3, which has a heavy Doric portico of square columns. The doorway has paneled pilasters supporting a simple entablature. There is a curious difference in character between the monumental front facade and the more intimate treatment of the side walls, a treatment which might reveal the influence of the Victorian movement.

Throughout the entire Ohio Valley are countless houses similar in character to the Hurst house, shown in Fig. 15-5. In many, the first clue to their lineage is revealed by the general proportions of the exterior and by the simplicity of treatment, which marks them as quite different from any version of the earlier Colonial examples. The simple cornice and the plain lintels and window sills betray the origin of these houses; if these elements are not sufficient proof, the Classical details around the doorway, as in Fig. 15-6, eliminate the last doubt about the ancestry of these structures.

BELOW THE OHIO

The southern states embraced the cause of Greek Revival architecture with a fervor even greater than in those states north and east of the Ohio. The South recognized it as a sentimental style but, nevertheless, one which reflected the intellectual and emotional life of those forceful days. The great plantations were being established,

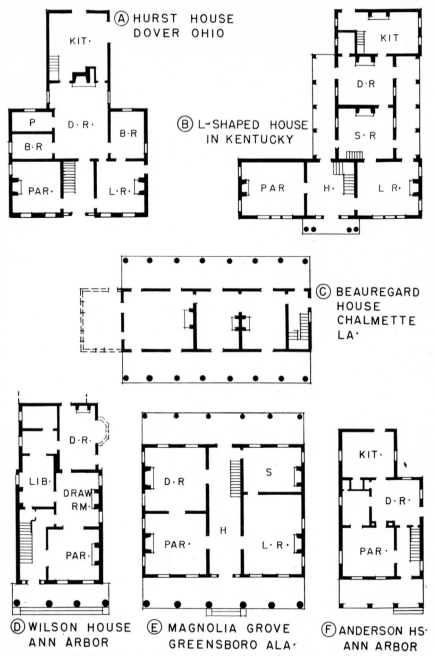

FIG. 15-7. The various plan types characteristic of the Greek Revival period are illustrated above. Shown are those with square, rectangular, T, and L shapes and those with and without porches.

Fig. 15-8. Melrose, Natchez vicinity, Mississippi. Late Greek Revival mansion, built in 1840. Heavy and monumental in character. Doric entrance portico.

family fortunes were being made, and a gay social life was developing against the background of slaves, cotton, and river packets. The Greek Revival movement occurred at a time most propitious for its acceptance by plantation-empire builders. Fortunately its physical characteristics permitted and even encouraged the development of the magnificent and spacious homes so necessary as the symbol of southern aristocracy.

The movement of the style was, as in the North, from the east to the west. The owners of tobacco and rice plantations and the citizens of the communities along the Atlantic seaboard had, by their encouragement of earlier expressions of the Classical, helped to pave the way for this new Greek architecture. Thomas Jefferson's Roman Doric porticoes had prepared the people for monumental architecture, while the two-story porch added to Mount Vernon late in the eighteenth century was probably the forerunner of similar porches or piazzas which became familiar features of the plantation homes of the Deep South.

The Greek Revival homes of the South constituted a barometer

FIG. 15-9. Rosalie, Natchez, Mississippi. Reminiscent of the Miles Brewton house, Charleston, Fig. 8-23. Two-story porch with pediment. Built between 1820 and 1823.

by which the influences of a culture and a climate could be read. The social life of the plantations was one of the deciding factors in the design of these houses built during the first half of the nineteenth century. As in Virginia, the plantations were large in area and the houses were far apart. Visits, as we have seen, were not of the short and casual type of New England but instead were protracted and formal. Entertaining was on a grand scale and large houses were necessary as a setting for these hospitable occasions. The rooms were spacious and impressive in appearance. Often they had large intercommunicating doors in order that a ball room could be fashioned on short notice. Hallways grew in size and importance, in keeping with the magnificence of the remainder of the house.

In addition to the influences just mentioned, climate also took a firm hand in shaping the form of these southern homes. In the Charleston area, as well as elsewhere along the coastal regions, the heat and humidity had much to do with the location of important elements of the house. In many homes of the early periods the low ground floor made it possible to raise the important activities asso-

FIG. 15-10. Roper house, Charleston, South Carolina. Mid nineteenth-century Greek Revival mansion. Monumental two-story porch across long side of house, with Ionic columns above ground floor.

ciated with the main floor above the damp soil. This is shown in Fig. 15-16. In Charleston, the weather directed the orientation of the dwellings so that the two- or three-story piazzas or galleries occurred along the south or west sides in order to protect the rooms from the midday sun and to provide a pleasant outdoor retreat, as shown in Fig. 15-10. Farther to the west and in the more formal town and plantation homes, large colonnades of tall Greek columns carried up two stories to form piazzas across the front and often around several sides of the house. In many instances a balcony with iron railings occurred at the second-floor level. These deep porches, while a definite part of the style, no doubt can trace their popularity to the influence of climate and to the desire for protection from the sun.

There was as much variety in house plans in the South as there was in the North. The temple type was a common one, but perhaps the most characteristic arrangement consisted of a simple square or rectangular area surrounded by porticoes, as in Fig. 15-7. On the first floor were to be found the hall, parlor, dining room, and perhaps a

FIG. 15-11. René Beauregard house, Chalmette, La. Mid nineteenth century. Influence of West Indies seen in curving roof. Heavy Greek Revival style with Doric columns.

FIG. 15-12. The Houmas, Burnside Plantation, Burnside, Louisiana. Ornate-type plantation house. Brick, two and half stories with cupola. Built about 1820 on 12,000-acre estate purchased from the Indians in 1774.

bedroom, together with the kitchen. Another common type was one which had the shape of a *T*, as in Fig. 15-7. The unit that projected toward the rear often had a two-story gallery on either side for out-door living. The *L*-shaped scheme was also characteristic of many of the homes of this period. In the rear wings of either type, various service rooms were located on the first floor, while guest rooms were placed on the second floor. The two-story porch which connected these rooms was a substitute for an enclosed hall, an acceptable ar-rangement because of the mildness of the climate.

In the South, both brick and wood found favor as building mate-rials. When wood was used for siding and for the columns, there was a conscious effort to imitate the stone architecture from which the style was derived, especially on the front of the house where an effort was made to impress the observer. In many of the homes throughout the South, extending all the way from the Gulf to Ken-tucky, brick was also used in the construction of the walls, permitting a pleasant contrast in color between the warmth of the brick and the whiteness of the columns and trim. However, since much of the brick of the southern states was made locally and was often soft and porous, many of the masonry walls have been covered with stucco for protec-tion from the weather.

On the exterior and interior of these southern homes were re-peated the same Greek details characteristic of the houses of the North. The Greek orders were used for the porticoes of the larger homes and for the porches and entrance doorways of the smaller houses. In New Orleans the Greek Revival came under the lingering influence of the earlier French and Spanish architecture. In the town houses Greek doorways and columns were combined with wrought-iron balconies of intricate design. In the great plantation area along the Gulf coast and reaching back into the Bayou country, there are, even today, many splendid examples of the typical plantation home with its Greek Doric portico, monumental entrance, and large win-dows. Houses of this type are illustrated in the René Beauregard house, Fig. 15-11, Burnside Plantation, Fig. 15-12, and Magnolia Grove, Fig. 15-13.

FIG. 15-13. (*opposite*). Magnolia Grove, Greensboro, Alabama. Built in 1830. Temple-type portico with Doric columns and pediment. Plan is shown in Fig. 15-7.

Fig. 15-14. The Shadows, New Iberia, Louisiana. 1830. Typical of Deep South.

Fig. 15-15. End of drawing room. Mantel with Greek moldings.

FIG. 15-16. Gorgas house, Tuscaloosa, Alabama. Built 1829 for University of Alabama. Residence since 1865.

FIG. 15-17. Detail of exterior stairway with ornate iron-work.

It is difficult to select any one or two of the many magnif.
houses built just before the Civil War for a description of their
tails and qualities. However, The Shadows, at New Iberia, Louisiai.
the main facade of which is shown in Fig. 15-14, is one of the truly
great homes of the period. Here we have all of the atmosphere of the
Deep South, a house in a setting of luxuriant vegetation and hangin,
moss recalling the romantic days of earlier generations. Here the
Doric columns and entablature are combined with brick walls to
produce a most pleasing effect. The drawing room, shown in Fig.
15-15, illustrates the restrained use of Greek details combined to retain the simplicity of the style.

Part THREE

THE ERA OF CONFUSION

MORE REVIVALS

Chapter 16

ROMANTICISM

INDUSTRIAL AMERICA

THE last half of the nineteenth century witnessed both the beginning and the end of the era of intensive westward expansion—the beginning in 1849, the end about 1890 when there were no more geographical frontiers. The significant happenings of the middle of the nineteenth century—the discovery of gold, the mass movement of people to the newly opened regions, the Civil War, the impetus given to the Industrial Revolution—all combined to create a turning point in the social, economic, and artistic life of the American people.

In time, it was the end of the period of colonial settlement and consolidation—a period that was peopled with merchants, artisans, shipbuilders, and farmers, all of whom depended largely on techniques and tools centuries old and most of whom lived in houses of Georgian and Classical derivation. In time, it was also the beginning of an era still composed largely of farmers and merchants operating on a larger scale than did their predecessors but one dominated by industrialists and businessmen, most of whom were using the tools of a new science and living in picturesquely ugly Gothic and Renaissance cottages and villas.

But even with the growth of cities, the social order of much of the nineteenth century belonged basically to the village and the town. The larger cities were still not far removed from the frontier; and the conspicuous difference between the city slicker and the country rube, so popular in the jokes of a few decades ago, had not yet been developed. The homes of the period reflected this proximity

215

to the grass roots of America: the homes in the towns and the towns themselves had not yet become cramped for space nor felt the impact of metropolitan devices and practices.

During the last half of the nineteenth century, America developed into a gigantic market for the purchase of raw materials and the sale of manufactured goods. The abundance of coal, iron ore, lumber, oil, flour, and meat and the presence of an industrial ingenuity to exploit them created a prosperity which gave rise to a new aristocracy of wealth with its accompanying architectural expression in homes and public buildings. The industrial development in the eastern half of the country was accompanied by the growth and decline of the cattle country in the prairie states west of the Mississippi. After the danger of Indian trouble was removed, Kansas City and other towns along the cattle trails grew overnight from frontier communities to busy cities rivaling many of those in the East. The open range beyond the cities was finally closed by the relentless advance of the farmer with his plow; the Middle West grew under the pressure of both an agrarian and industrial economic order. Here was the scene of frenzied building.

Much of the last half of the nineteenth century, during which the Gothic and Renaissance revivals dominated the design of domestic architecture, was characterized by complexity and confusion. It was a confusion that accompanied rapid progress in the design and use of the tools belonging to the industrial culture of America. It was a confusion that grew from overnight improvements in the machinery for living; it was marked by speculation in land, economic inflation, and the establishment of huge fortunes. Railroads penetrated the isolated areas and brought the United States together as an economic unit as other factors had done in the political sense. No longer were there large isolated regions completely removed from the influences of the rest of the country. The crude customs, dress, and houses of the frontier began to disappear, to be replaced by a greater standardization of interests, living conditions, and ideas about the construction of homes.

The social order that emerged from the villages, towns, and cities during the nineteenth century reflected the background of conflicting contrasts of wealth and poverty, of crudeness and good manners, of ugliness and beauty. The material progress that came with such a rush encouraged rapid changes in attitudes and practices. People began to work under new conditions and to live—with reference to family life, recreation, and education—according to the influences of the new developments in science and industry.

RECREATION

From the days of the Pilgrims—with their long hours of physical labor, the lack of reading matter, the preponderance of illiteracy, and the absence of adequate lighting—there had been a steady improvement in the recreational opportunities of the American people. However, it was not until the machine produced the printing press, gas and electric illumination, and commercial entertainment, that the drudgery of hard work was relieved by anything other than the simplest kind of recreation. But even with these changes, much of the social life of middle-class America was still found in the church and church activities. Without doubt some denominations were losing their hold upon the activities of people as compared to the Colonial days but, nevertheless, the church continued to be the scene of many of the concerts and lectures. The movies and organized sports had not yet appeared to make a challenge for the leisure time of the American people.

Mass participation in athletic, recreational, and cultural pursuits, so common today, was still in its infancy. If sporting blood existed in the male members of the family, it must be satisfied surreptitiously; the men might sneak away to a race, a prize fight, or a ball game. The approved amusements for the entire family consisted of picnics, socials, bicycling, and buggy rides. Dancing and card playing were permitted for those whose religious beliefs were liberal. Perhaps the most popular sport was that of bicycling. Bicycles filled the paths and parks, endangering the physical well-being of the participants and the dignity of the pedestrians. As well-paved streets were built to connect the new homes of the period, the sport of cycling was encouraged still more; even the country roads beckoned to the adventurous.

But in spite of the popularity of certain sports—of football, baseball, rowing, golf, and tennis—it was a period of unwholesome prudishness. Physical weakness and poor health were marks of

Fig. 16-1. A late nineteenth-century interior, showing a typical "den" with all of the confused coziness of the period. Here are the familiar objects of art—the pictures, lamps, vases, and portieres—combined with a Renaissance-type mantel.

distinction which set aside the young men and women of the middle and upper classes as fragile creatures living in a romantic world. Heavy meals at breakfast, dinner, and supper probably contributed in a real way to shortness of breath and to bad complexion. At the best, dress had not yet reached the simple character of the present generation. Long skirts and button shoes, sailor hats and sleeve supporters, and all types of heavy clothing hampered young and old in school, sports, or business. The homes of the period, with their poor planning and with their interiors crowded with uncomfortable furniture and useless bric-a-brac, reflected the lack of understanding of the conveniences of life in terms of present-day standards.

If the decades previous to the Civil War—when the Greek Revival style of architecture dominated the design of our homes—saw the beginning of present-day America, the last half of the century witnessed the development of material things already conceived. Many of the things that we now regard as the product of the twentieth century received their start in the nineteenth century. We might not wish to return to the inconveniences of the horse-drawn street cars, pitchers and wash basins, board sidewalks, false-front stores, gas lights, cuspidors, gramaphones, and patent medicine, but it was from these humble beginnings that many of our present-day comforts and aids were developed. The gas light gave way to electricity, the horse and buggy was replaced by the automobile, while the magic lantern was succeeded by the movies and television. Our grandparent's limited diet has been improved through the development of canned, processed, and frozen foods; the life expectancy of a few generations ago has been raised by a more scientific approach to the matter of health.

These improvements have taken place within the lifetime of our elders. For those who now live in the twentieth century, colonial days are two centuries ago in the dim past but, for these same persons, the Victorian era, with all of its ugliness and inconveniences, is only yesterday. From this yesterday came the things which, through development, have helped make the mechanics for living in the home more productive of pleasure, convenience, and comfort.

PALACES AND COTTAGES

By the last half of the nineteenth century, American culture was settling into a familiar pattern. Three classes of people were emerging as conspicuous segments of the social order—the aristocracy of money or intellect, the middle class with its various gradations, and the poor in both wealth and education. Speculation in land led to speculation in stocks; fortunes were quickly made and often quickly lost. Wealth was displayed by lavish spending; the social world of the long-established merchant, shipowner, and statesman was besieged by the newly rich industrialist. The plutocrats of nineteenth-century America were no different from the *nouveaux riches* of other countries and ages. They had come so recently from the mines, the forests, and the mills that, in order to wear the badge of distinction, they had to dress, live, and act—consciously and deliberately—the part of moneyed nobility. They built magnificent palaces and bought ornate art objects to create a setting for their expensive and sometimes bacchanalian social gatherings. They turned to Europe for inspiration, and it was not long until the simplicity of Colonial and Classical architecture was buried under an avalanche of imported chateaux, manor houses, and castles—some archeologically correct in their design,

Fig. 16-2. W. K. Vanderbilt residence on Fifth Avenue, New York, which was a typical expression of the new-found wealth of the American businessman. The inspiration for the treatment came from the Loire Valley.

others created as monstrosities of meaningless ornament. With their new-found wealth, the wealthy purchased the architecture and the superficial veneer of a social culture that the people of Europe had acquired over centuries of development.

The homes of the period naturally were a true index to the financial status of the various economic groups. The house of the wealthy man was likely to be a huge and ornate structure of brick or stone; his parlors and drawing rooms were usually filled with carved woodwork, imported marble sculpture, and original oil paintings. The poor—represented by the slum dwellers of the cities, the tenant farmers of the South and West, and the immigrants who furnished the cheap labor of the industrial communities—lived in crowded flats on the side streets of our cities or in shacks on marginal land in our rural districts.

THE MIDDLE CLASS

It is to the middle class of the nineteenth century, and not to the representatives of contrasting groups, that we turn for a picture of family life and domestic architecture that we can most easily understand. We read about the spectacular doings of the wealthy, the palaces that they built, the lawn parties and formal balls that they gave, and the numerous servants whom they employed. However, this represented only a small, even though conspicuous, part of American life. All of nineteenth-century America did not drink champagne from a lady's slipper, wear necklaces costing a small fortune, or live in magnificent chateaux. Instead, most of the population was composed of the substantial people of the nation—of the small-town merchant, the doctor, the lawyer, the skilled artisan, and the office worker. These people lived in fairly modest homes, Fig. 16-3, and led relatively simple existences as compared to those who resided on Fifth Avenue. The lives of the middle class have meaning to those of us in the twentieth century.

The homes of the middle class, as well as those of the wealthy, reflected the social changes brought about by the influx of unskilled workers from Europe. There was a new attitude in the cities toward manual labor. The man of frontier America had been a Jack-of-all-trades. He could work in the fields, in the shop, and in the home. He could build houses and fences and make plows and furniture. Now it came to be beneath the dignity of even the middle class, as it always had been of the wealthy, to perform the more menial tasks. Increased financial freedom brought a greater demand for household servants, to be followed by a more elaborate form of family and social life. The work of the husband was relieved by a gardener and coachman, the work of the wife by a cook and a maid. The old relationship between the mistress and the hired girl no longer existed. Although the hired girl had probably been one of the neighbor's daughters, the new cook was a foreigner from an inferior social class.

Thus the substantial, middle-class citizens of America began to keep servants and put on airs. The mistress of the family, encouraged by her husband's improved financial status and by the new freedom from dependence on the neighbors for domestic help, usually demanded a house worthy of the new furniture, rugs, and decorative bric-a-brac. As is inevitable in most periods of architectural development, the homes of these middle-class families were often only smaller copies, in cheaper materials, of the ornate homes of the wealthy. Again they followed the lead of those whom they imitated;

Fig. 16-3. In contrast to the chateaux on Fifth Avenue and the manor houses on Long Island were the countless more modest homes of the middle class, with limited ostentation and ornateness.

their taste in matters artistic and architectural left much to be desired. Their parlor floors were covered with ingrain carpets instead of imported rugs and their furniture was machine-made of walnut or oak instead of mahogany and marble. These middle-class families may have looked with longing eyes at the comforts of those who built their villas at Newport and Saratoga but, with their modest financial status, they were forced to lead the lives of average Americans. Middle-class family life and domestic architecture responded to the impact of this slowly unfolding American pattern—a pattern that reflected the entire gamut of background influences from those of the raw frontier to those of the industrial city.

In the middle-class home of the nineteenth century, the dining room was usually the most important room in the house, just as the "hall" was in the Early American home or the kitchen is today in the farmhouse. Here were served the three complete meals considered necessary in those days and here the entire family lingered after supper for conversation, studying, mending, and other domestic activities. In the Victorian days of the last half of the century there was a closer relationship or connection between this dining room and the source of the food supply than that existing today. This was, of course, before the day of complete mechanization, before food processing and the marriage of science and nature. In those days the dinner table was close to the home garden or the farm. This very proximity —before the development of the refrigerator car or airplane to bring foods normally out of season—affected the eating habits of a nation and the design of the kitchen and dining room. Food came in bulk form—in bushels instead of ounces—demanded large kitchens for its preparation, and encouraged sumptuous meals for the family gatherings in the dining room. The heavy appetites of our Victorian ancestors may not be ignored when we discuss the influences of family life on the character of houses.

But the eating habits of America gradually changed. As cities grew in size and as public transportation carried workers farther from home, businessmen began taking the noon meal away from the family dining room. In addition, lunchrooms were established in the schools and the housewife was released even more from the burden of preparing the heavy dinner in the middle of the day. This new freedom was the forerunner of other releases from household drudgery which ultimately had their effect on family life and on the design of domestic shelter. In taking the noon meal away from home, men discovered that mental work could be performed better after a lighter repast, and the idea of lunch came into being. Perhaps, for the first time, diet and healthful living were related; it is possible that the more casual attitude toward dining, characteristic of the contemporary scene, and the growing merger of the dining space with other living areas had their beginnings in the Victorian era. There was no sudden change in house planning—only a gradual loss of importance of the isolated dining room until the present rush to subordinate the dining area to that related to rest and relaxation.

With much of the family life of the middle nineteenth century carried on around the dining room table or at times in a living room, the parlor often assumed a kind of musty dignity. This room—with its marble fireplace, carved tables, horsehair upholstered sofas and chairs, whatnots, and framed mottoes—was usually reserved for company and formal occasions. The inefficiency of early heating systems and the lack of insulation encouraged the use of carpets in the parlor and other important rooms, carpets which covered the entire floor. Under the carpet was placed straw, matting, or paper, which had to be renewed at intervals; house cleaning in the spring was an event when mother and the hired girl moved everything out into the yard for a complete renovation. This was the day that father stayed at the office or in the store as late as possible in order to escape the confusion and short tempers accompanying this upheaval.

Other differences existed between the homes of the Victorian period and those of today. Then the kitchen was likely to be removed some distance from the dining room and was still a poorly arranged room equipped with the inefficient appliances of the period. The bedrooms on the second floor were usually alike in their lack of proper facilities and furnishings for comfortable sleep according to present-day standards. Mother and father had the best front room, since the noise of traffic was not then a factor, while the other rooms were assigned to other members of the family in the order of their ages. Bedrooms were not scientifically planned as they are now and they had few closets or other provisions for convenience and comfort. Bathrooms, where they existed, were usually dark and unpleasant spaces with little hint of twentieth-century glamour. The attached garage, so common today, was not dreamed of—instead, the polite stable–carriage house with its weathervane was a conspicuous part of the establishments of those who could afford a span of spanking bays.

Chapter 17

THE GOTHIC REVIVAL

THE ROOTS IN EUROPE

SINCE the period of frenzied industrial and financial activity that followed the Civil War caught the newly rich class and also the less wealthy—though perhaps more tranquil—middle class without the "culture" that they so ardently desired, it was necessary for them to take hasty steps to correct this deficiency. The physical confidence that developed with the acquisition of wealth had not been accompanied by an equal confidence in the simple art and architecture inherited from the previous generation. In the interest of speed, it was necessary to borrow from abroad. The people of America, just before and after the midcentury period, in turning to England and the continent for the purchase of a ready-made culture, found the Industrial Revolution in full swing; they found, perhaps to their relief, a full-fledged revolt against the Classicism of the preceding decades.

In England these Americans found a country ruled by Victoria Regina in matters of politics, manners, and public taste—by Victoria and her lieutenants in the persons of Dickens, Scott, Ruskin, George Eliot, Tennyson, and the Brownings. These intellectuals set the pattern in literature and thought—a pattern with the emphasis, not upon the ideals of Greece and Rome as was the case during the earlier decades of the nineteenth century, but rather upon the more poignant sentimentalities of nature and the common man. These American tourists and also those who stayed at home were drawn into the orbit of this galaxy of creators of English culture; they could accept with greater confidence the philosophies of Lowell, Whittier, and Longfellow. In the field of art they found the paintings of Land-

FIG. 17-1. The Great Hall, Penshurst Place, Kent, 1388. In this impressive room, with its timber roof supported by pointed arches, are gathered the lord and lady and their guests to watch the boisterous antics of the retainers as they bring in the Yule log. The romantic appeal of this period helped to popularize the Gothic Revival movement in this country.

seer and the marbles of Canova, together with the works of the pre-Raphaelites represented by Burne-Jones and Rossetti, all appealing to the emotions rather than the mind. In the field of architecture they found Pugin and other draftsmen with drawings of Gothic manor houses and Sir Charles Barry with his Houses of Parliament, representatives of a romantic movement in contrast with the exactness of the Classical. This combination of culture, art, and architecture formed the background for the Victorian period in English and American life, a period that was synonymous with confusion in creative activities and prudishness in ways of living. The Victorian influence laid a heavy hand on family life and shelter and, in architecture, prevented the continuation of the simplicity of the Greek Revival.

The writings of Queen Victoria's lieutenants were as popular in America as they were in England; for the many who could not afford a summer among the manor houses of Kent or the chateaux of the Loire, an excursion through the printed pages was a satisfactory substitute for first-hand impressions. But in spite of the imposing list of people who were responsible for the literature, morals, and art of the Victorian period, it was Ruskin, more than any other one individual, who exerted the greatest influence on the development of the Gothic Revival movement in this country. His books were received in the United States with even more enthusiasm than abroad and his philosophy left its imprint long after his time. Through the increased use of the printed word, the great middle class, even more than the wealthy, was indoctrinated with the teachings of Ruskin as presented in his *Seven Lamps of Architecture* and other books.

Ruskin was interested in humanity in general and in the common man in particular. He believed that the academic quality of the Classical style was unrelated to the technology of the Industrial Revolution; and, as a solution to the evils created by the machine, he proposed the adoption of the spirit and details of the Venetian Gothic.

The coming of the machine had improved the physical well-being of Americans but had neglected their spiritual salvation; Ruskin became a savior in matters artistic. Under his influence, people retreated into the past and drew upon the romance of the Middle Ages, thus hoping to escape the rawness of their industrial cities. Perhaps the informality of the Gothic—whether Venetian, French, or English—carried some suggestion of battlemented towers with knights in armor and ladies in waiting. The banquets in the great halls and the jousting bouts beyond the moats took nineteenth-century Americans in mind and spirit away from the smoke-laden atmosphere of the factory towns. Whatever may have been the chief instrument in the change, the Gothic style, gaining a foothold here before the middle of the century and lasting until the last quarter, replaced the Greek Revival in the hearts of the American people and became the popular type of treatment for the exteriors of the homes of the period.

The homes of the Gothic Revival period varied in their adherence to the exact details of the medieval style as they came under the influence of the Victorian movement; it is, therefore, not accurate to speak disparagingly of all the picturesque architecture inspired by the castles and manor houses of England. In fact, the churches, especially those designed by such architects as James Renwick and Richard Upjohn, were academically correct in the use of details even though they were somewhat mechanical in general character. In a like manner, the early houses of the period built before the middle of the century, and also some of the later ones, followed rather faithfully the composition and spirit of the better works of Gothic England. The buildings were at least interesting and charming; though sentimental in their appeal and impractical in their planning, they were not displeasing to the eye.

THE MACHINE

However, archeological correctness was not to last for long; the development of the jigsaw and the lathe gave the Victorian designer and workman a new freedom without an accompanying restraint of good taste. In much of the domestic architecture of the last half of the nineteenth century, confusion and ugliness were consistently and conspicuously present; the homes of the wealthy, the middle class, and even the poor were touched in varying degrees with this blight of poorly designed pointed arches, ornate gables, steep roofs, and jigsaw ornaments.

Much of the blame for the confused architecture of the Victorian period can be laid at the door of the machine. In the days of colonial development, the carpenter-architect created graceful columns and capitals and delicate moldings and carvings; he executed them with a skill which revealed his sense of design and his love of materials. The Industrial Revolution meant the end of this fine craftsmanship. The ease with which the machine could turn out the furniture, utensils, tools, and architectural details necessary for nineteenth-century life spelled the doom of the artisan who worked skillfully and understandingly in wood, metal, and stone. The craftsman who took pride in his craving and joining could not compete with the cheap imitations of the machine which satisfied the debased public taste of the time. The lathe and band saw could cut out stylized and ugly decorations for the porch, gable, or stairway. The furnace and the mold could create cast-iron substitutes for wood and stone. The machine could produce but the operator had not yet learned about the relationship between art and mass production. It was not until well into the twentieth century that the designer began to make the machine the servant of the creative artist.

There are, of course, many examples still extant of the Gothic

17-2. From Victorian England and Gothic manor houses came the inspiration for the pointed arches, octagonal towers with crenelated tops, and finials with foliated decorations which are incorporated in this nineteenth-century American home.

17-3. "Greystone," mid nineteenth-century Gothic Revival house near Pevely, Mo. The steep roof with decorative bargeboards and terminating finials and the clustered chimneys are very characteristic of the medieval style. This house suggests the heavy-handed romance of the Victorian era.

Revival style but too often they are only ghosts of the past. A few of the fine homes of the period have been well kept and stand today behind ornate iron fences in the midst of spreading lawns. They may be occupied by remnants of old families making their last stand, in an atmosphere of lavender and old lace, against the encroachments of the changing world. Many more have lost the battle against deterioration and find themselves in areas given over to rooming houses and used-car lots. They are occupied by another and less fortunate generation for whom they furnish inadequate and outmoded shelter. The more modest homes of the Victorian period, built at a time when poor planning and ugly exteriors discouraged longevity, have often suffered a similar fate. They too go unnoticed amidst the blight and confusion of our towns and cities.

COMPLEXITY AND CONFUSION

It is possible, therefore, to secure a more accurate picture of life and architecture during the last half of the nineteenth century by turning to the books of the period which describe the currently popular house designs. Their very titles are revealing. These books were published as *Rural Cottages, Cottage Villas, The Gothic Villa,* and other equally romantic and descriptive titles. The houses illustrated ranged from the simple cottages in the country to the magnificent villas in Newport and Saratoga. During most of the Victorian period, the common characteristic of these houses was a liberal and romantic interpretation of Gothic and, later, Italian Renaissance massing and details. In many instances, Chinese and Moorish motifs were thrown in for good measure; in most examples, picturesqueness was the keynote of the design. The architects who published these nineteenth-century handbooks took many liberties with the architecture of Pugin and Palladio; but, in spite of their efforts to bring beauty and romance into the lives of the American people, domestic architecture was generally drab, dingy, and monotonous.

On the whole, the homes of the period were heavy and awkward in their external silhouette and restless and confused in the composition of their exterior and interior details. Their picturesque exteriors were wood, brick, or stone, the latter composed of granite or brownstone laid up with rough faces or in regular ashlar with smooth sur-

FIG. 17-4. Here is a variety of architectural forms and types of treatment—a Victorian villa with ornate porches, towers, turrets, and dormers. The basic influence is Renaissance rather than the Gothic shown in Fig. 17-2.

faces. Regardless of the treatment, an unpleasant mechanical effect was likely to be achieved. The sensitiveness of the craftsman had been replaced by the crassness of the machine.

The houses of the period, with their elaborate entrances, porches, and piazzas, ranged in character from mechanically correct stone structures with Gothic two- or four-centered arches, buttresses, and undercut moldings to the more intimate jigsaw variations in wood. Countless homes of this period displayed a fondness for steep gables with ornately decorated barge boards, as shown in Fig. 17-2, together with clustered chimneys, bay windows, and elaborate towers and turrets. In short, the picturesque architecture of the last half of the century was quite the opposite in appearance to the simple buildings of the first half.

The planning of these cottages and villas also lost the simplicity of the Colonial and Greek Revival styles. The rooms increased in number and their shape became more varied than in the former examples, Fig. 21-13C. Bay windows and turrets helped to create rooms that departed in shape from the simple rectangle and that included awkward corners and outlines. The relationship between rooms was often based on the desire for effect rather than convenient use. There was little economy of space or effort, especially in the larger homes where the presence of servants offset the effects of poor planning. The kitchen as we have seen, was often removed some distance from the dining room; it was usually located beyond a butler's pantry, at the end of a corridor, or even in the basement. In addition, most of the other conveniences of present-day homes were missing. Plumbing was primitive, heating was inefficient and dirty, circulatory paths were poorly developed, and closets were generally lacking.

If we refer again to the books on house design, we can secure from the title page additional information about the plans of these homes. The Rural Cottage was an ambitious structure with four bedrooms; the Country House had a library and parlor; the Irregular House with Kitchen Wing had a kitchen work area separated from the dining room by a corridor; the Wooden Villa with Towers was a picturesque, unsymmetrical house; while the Stone Villa was a Gothic castle with drawing rooms, parlors, boudoirs, dining room, and servants' rooms on the first floor and magnificent chambers on the second level.

If it were necessary to summarize our impressions of the Gothic or Renaissance villa of the Victorian era, we would picture an ornate house with porches, piazzas, balconies, and towers, as in Fig. 17-4. The house would be set well back from the street, and the front lawn might be adorned with the familiar cast-iron deer. A sweeping drive would lead to the porte-cochere where a span of horses and a Victoria waited for the lady of the house with her high button shoes,

FIG. 17-5. Gothic Revival house at Red Beach, Maine. Decorative bargeboard.

FIG. 17-6. House at Calais, Maine, showing use of Carpenter's Gothic.

Fig. 17-7. Austin house, Paris, Illinois. A frame house of the mid nineteenth century. The vertical siding and bracketed cornice above the door show the Victorian influence in the Gothic Revival treatment.

bustled skirt, and frilled parasol. This is, of course, a picture of the homes of the more wealthy, but those of the middle class were, in general, only smaller and less ornate copies of the larger houses. The confusion of the architectural treatment seemed to vary in direct ratio with the wealth of the owner and the size of the house, but the modest homes, while affording less space for meaningless details, were equally ugly in their proportions and choice of materials.

In a desire to condemn bad taste, it is very easy to dwell at length on the ugliness of the Victorian movement in art, furnishings, and architecture—upon the Eastlake period with its welter of angular furniture, sentimental accessories, and jigsaw ornament. In doing this, however, we are pointing to the worst of the style and overlooking some of the more charming examples, such as the houses shown in Figs. 17-5 and 17-6, which are delightfully interesting in their use of Gothic decoration. These interpretations were sometimes called Steamboat Gothic and Carpenter's Gothic, titles that indicate the wide departure from the ideals of the Classical Revival.

18

THE MELTING POT

As America became the melting pot for the many racial groups that came to these shores, it also became, in the late nineteenth century, the scene of the battle of the styles. Here was the struggle between the Victorian Gothic, the French and Italian Renaissance, the Romanesque, and other variations of traditional architecture. Here was also the melting pot of materials and colors. The buildings of Colonial and Greek Revival days were composed in a simple manner with reference to the use of materials, but now the pot began to boil over with the many ingredients. Brick, tile, stone, terra cotta, mosaics, and stained glass were combined in one building with many colors and textures. The result was a restless, overdecorated architecture which continued until the restraining influences of the Classicism of the Chicago World's Fair, or the Columbian Exposition, in 1893.

THE THIRD EMPIRE

As the decades of the late nineteenth century passed, the tide of American tourists flooding Europe turned from England to France. Here they increased their architectural vocabulary by visiting the medieval and Renaissance buildings of earlier centuries and also the current versions born of French creative genius. Here they saw the chateaux along the Loire at Chambord, Blois, and Chenonceaux and the earlier cliff-like castle at Pierrefonds. But their most vivid recollections were of Paris—of the Library of St. Genevieve, the Hôtel de Ville, the Opera House, and the many magnificent buildings along the Place de la Concorde. They remembered the rich exterior treat-

FIG. 18-1. Grand stairway, Paris Opera House, 1861-1874, where the nineteenth-century American tourists came under the spell of the magnificence of the Third Empire.

FIG. 18-2. Pavillon Turgot of the Louvre, Paris, 1857-1857. This type of ornate treatment was repeated in many of the buildings erected in the United State during the late nineteenth century.

ment and the monumental scale of these structures; they remembered the steep roofs, dormer windows, and circular and square towers, together with the rustication, carving, sculpture, and ornate columns and entablatures. They remembered and acted on these remembrances.

Thus these travelers brought back to this country the belief that copies of the magnificent buildings erected for the aristocracy of France during the centuries of the power and glory of her kings would be the proper setting for the social activities of the new American aristocracy of wealth and power. It is no wonder, therefore, that the late nineteenth-century homes of the wealthy were smaller editions of the palaces and chateaux of France and that the homes of the middle class were copied after the designs of their more fortunate neighbors. The Gothic cottages and villas were repeated in plan only, with a different kind of exterior treatment. Gothic entrances, windows, carving, and roofs gave way to Renaissance

Fig. 18-3. House at Eastport, Maine, showing the influence of French architecture in the use of a mansard roof with dormers. The decorative brackets at the entrance and under the cornice reveal the influence of the Victorian movement.

counterparts. The plans of the villas were large in scale and complex in composition; the exteriors were informally picturesque with their towers, turrets, balconies, and oriels. In some, the mansard roofs with iron cresting, the heavy walls with rusticated and vermiculated quoins, the ornate columns and broken pediments, and great variety of pseudo-Renaissance details were conspicuous features. This complexity of treatment is well illustrated in the Morse-Libby house, shown in Fig. 18-4. A more modest version of the French style, with considerable evidence of Victorian influence in the use of brackets in the cornice and at the entrance, is presented in the house at Eastport, Maine, Fig. 18-3. The interiors of the large and ornate houses usually repeated the character of the exteriors; they were at least as rich in ornamentation and as monumental in scale. They were the antithesis of the homelike and livable rooms of the Colonial period, or of the great manor houses of Virginia, as seen in Fig. 6-16.

As was the case with the Gothic Revival, the purity of form and detail of the French Revival varied with the extent to which the Victorian movement exerted an influence. Some buildings followed very closely the design and character of the French inspirations, while others were much modified, usually to their detriment, by the use of incongruous decorative elements. Unfortunately the desire for ostentation was usually not denied.

MISCELLANEA

One of the well-known minor types of treatment was generally recognized as Carpenter's Victorian or Carpenter's Colonial, a style developed without the restraint and sensitiveness of the carpenters and craftsmen of colonial days. Here was a mixture of balusters, porches, columns, bracketed cornices, and cottage windows with colored glass transoms—all combined with little knowledge of good massing and composition, (Figs. 18-6 and 18-7). Here was evidence of the influence of the machine, which produced turned porch posts and spindle-like ornaments to create typical American middle-class homes in all parts of the country. The style became a popular one around the turn of the century and, as represented by the white frame houses still conspicuous along the older residential streets of our smaller communities, is worthy of notice among architectural movements.

Another architectural movement of the late nineteenth century, which had some influence on the design of houses, was that of the Romanesque, a style inspired largely by the efforts of H. H. Richardson. While Richardson is best known for Trinity Church in Boston, his creative imagination is also well expressed in his public buildings and in the houses that he designed. In those of brick or stone, there was much use of heavy round arches and many other details characteristic of the Romanesque period. However, it was in his houses of frame construction that he displayed his best efforts in domestic architecture. Here the shingle walls, surmounted by broad roofs and abutted by wide piazzas, were copied for many decades by those who were intrigued by the picturesque massing of this style.

It is unfortunate that so much of America was built when the influences from Europe were of such a baroque nature, when public taste was at such a low ebb, and when the machine in its infancy had not yet felt the influence of the present contemporary movement in design. Many of the dwellings of the period are now in blighted marginal areas given over to nondescript retail sections; while others,

FIG. 18-4. Morse-Libby house, Portland, Maine. Baroque Renaissance architecture.

FIG. 18-5. Interior of music room, showing ornate treatment.

Fig. 18-6. Here are the familiar turned porch posts of the Carpenter's Colonial style, carrying an open band of ornament, above which is an orthodox cornice with the usual projecting moldings.

Fig. 18-7. A double porch, showing the use of gingerbread decorations so typical of the product of the machine. Although this style belongs to the past, it is still as American as is Thanksgiving.

in the form of row houses, flats and stores, or detached homes, have become the slums of our towns and cities. In some instances the ambitious but outmoded structures are still maintained in the grand manner by the descendants of the founders of the pork, coal, and brewing dynasties; while the more modest examples, through the protection of proper zoning and the use of paint and repairs, are serving in a somewhat inadequate manner as the homes of the present-day middle- or lower-income groups. Whatever the fate of the representatives of Victorian Gothic, French Renaissance, American Romanesque, and all the mongrel derivations, we must realize that they constitute a large proportion of the homes of twentieth-century America. We may include them only reluctantly in our discussions of domestic architecture but we cannot ignore their existence. They reflect an important and inescapable period of our social and economic development and, as permanent records of our nineteenth-century culture, must be part of "shelter for living."

Part FOUR
THE PRESENT CENTURY
TRADITION AND FUNCTION

Chapter 19

ECLECTICISM

THE LIFE OF THE PERIOD

IF the period of American life just prior to the Civil War saw the beginning of many of our present-day techniques and institutions, and if the Industrial Revolution which followed witnessed the partial development of these aids to living, it is equally true that the twentieth century has brought the perfection of many of the things that make contemporary life efficient and comfortable and permit a scientific approach to the planning of homes. But let us remember that we have just come from the last remnants of Victorian restrictions to the freedom of modern thought and action. Early in this century we were still wearing full skirts, sailor hats, and sleeve supporters for polite bicycling and a modest kind of tennis. The fashionable garb for automobile travel consisted of dusters, veils, and goggles. A generation ago girls were still in pinafores and boys in little Lord Fauntleroy suits. Generally, the houses of those days were just as uncomfortable and illogical as was the dress; they were confused in plan and ugly in appearance. Today, these styles in dress, travel, and architecture are outmoded but they are still lingering memories of the years following the Gay Nineties.

The material progress of this nation since the beginning of the century has, in many respects, been phenomenal but it has not been consistent in all types of human endeavor. We are using the tools of tomorrow while living in the homes of yesterday. Science has given us efficient machines for transportation, manufacturing, and entertainment; science has developed functional structures to shelter the instruments for these activities. In general, however, our cities and our homes have not kept pace with other forms of physical development. Our cities, cast in an inflexible mold which defies major changes and improvements, are not geared to the ever increasing tempo of contemporary life. In their youth, many American communities must have been charming and adequate as places in which to live and work. But today, age is all too apparent in the outmoded gridiron system of streets designed for the horse-and-buggy traffic of yesterday. The central business district is threatened by decentralization while the fringes are suffering from blight and decay. Domestic architecture has suffered from this confusion; the practice of good home planning has been discouraged by traffic congestion, poor subdivision design, inadequate zoning laws, and outmoded building codes.

As a partial relief from the effects of out-of-date patterns and practices, city planning is making a belated effort to correct some of the evils of urban life; but, like remodeling a house, the results are expensive and only partly satisfactory. The nuisances of smoke, noise, and confusion are being partially eliminated, while traffic is unsnarled by the construction of expressways and the improvement of public transportation. A better relationship is being established between work places and living spaces—between factories, offices, and homes. In addition, new communities are blossoming overnight into full-blown maturity without going through the stages of frontier growth. Garden cities or green-belt communities with well-planned neighborhoods or small component parts, shopping centers with off-street parking, and homes built around the necessary recreational facilities promise to be free from many of the disadvantages of older cities. The homes of tomorrow, in the replanned communities of the future, will reflect the new concern for the house as "a machine for living in" which has been humanized by providing for the spiritual qualities of a daily existence.

The entire pattern of American culture has felt the impact of the dominance of the machine in our social and economic order. Mass production manufactures and modern advertising sells countless appliances for everyday living. An article is created and a market is found; or, in reverse, a need is discovered and is immediately satisfied by the ingenuity of designers, engineers, manufacturers, and distributors. Transportation and communication have all but eliminated the last evidence of provincialism in America. New styles in clothing are developed in New York, new movies produced in Hollywood, new homes built in Florida; they soon become the fashion in Elmira, Sioux City, and Walla Walla. The housewife in a small mountainous settlement of Tennessee may have the same refrigerator in her kitchen and the same permanent wave in her hair as her sister in Chicago. In earlier days, Colonial, Greek Revival, and Victorian architecture spread rather slowly by trails, rivers, and railroads to the more distant communities; in recent decades, prospective homeowners have been exposed—by magazines, movies, and vacation trips—to a continuous panorama of Colonial, English, and Modern houses. Too often the emphasis has been on style rather than on the influences of climate, materials, local customs, and family needs. As a result there has been a monotonous similarity between the homes of all parts of the country —a monotony of styles revived and copied.

THE MANY STYLES

To the method of designing homes with the forms of various traditional styles has been applied the term "Eclecticism." Eclecticism may be defined as the choosing of doctrines (of architecture) from various systems of thought to form an acceptable practice. We need only to examine the houses built during the last half century to realize that the borrowing of architectural styles of the past has been and still remains the acceptable practice of many American architects, builders, and homeowners.

It is obvious that the most conspicuous characteristics of the Eclectic movement are imitation and adaptation. The latter action has been the one redeeming feature of domestic architecture as far as progress and improvement are concerned. It was inevitable that American regard for convenience and comfort would demand the modification of some of the undesirable features of a stylistically correct plan and exterior. Improvements in heating, lighting, and sanitation resulted in greater freedom in planning and design. The compactness of the streamlined train, the luxury liner, the automobile, the airplane, and the rocket ship has been transferred to the kitchen, lavatory, bathroom, and laundry, and promises to affect even the living quarters of the home. The need for workers in the factory

FIG. 19-1. Various phases of Colonial architecture are expressed in this house, with its walls of field stone and painted siding, shuttered windows, Classical entrance with pilasters, and second-floor overhang with pendant drops reminiscent of the Early American.

and office has taken the maiden aunt of the Victorian era out of the kitchen and has thus decreased the number of workers in this domestic work space. The latter has now become a laboratory, planned to be economical of time and effort. These changes in ways of living and their influences upon house design are continuing at an ever accelerating rate; and, with the further encouragement of the non-traditional movement, the homes that were copied so slavishly from European styles are rapidly losing their popularity.

We shall return to the late nineteenth century for an event that brought an end to the battle of the styles as waged at that time and gave impetus to twentieth-century Eclecticism. Prior to the Chicago World's Fair of 1893, the various interpretations of the Victorian held the popular fancy; but, with the publicity given to the buildings of imperial Rome which surrounded the lagoons adjacent to Lake Michigan, the nineteenth-century period of utter confusion came to a conclusion. The Romantic movement, which had leaned so heavily on the poetical reverence for the past, gave way to this Classical influence and finally to the rebirth of the almost-forgotten Colonial style. But the domination of the Classical and the Colonial was short

Fig. 19-2. A large house designed in the manner of the English medieval style, with steep roof, field-stone walls, pointed arches, and stucco and half-timber treatment as decoration.

lived. The Colonial style was soon joined by adaptations of other periods and once again English cottages and manor houses, French farmhouses and minor chateaux, and Italian and Spanish villas appeared in American suburbs. They did not appear sequentially, each in its own period, but, instead, concurrently, as an architectural rash upon the face of the country. Thus the Victorian confusion of the nineteenth century was succeeded by the Eclectic confusion of the twentieth century, and the battle of the styles still continues.

Unfortunately for those who are sensitive to the principles of creative design and to the requirements of good planning, many of the less expensive homes built since the turn of the century have been nondescript or ugly in appearance and either mediocre or poor in plan arrangement. Those individuals who could not afford or did not want the services of an architect depended on the stock plans furnished by various companies and organizations or on the ready-built homes offered by the less reliable of the speculative builders. As a result, much of suburban America has been built by those whose conception of architecture has not been based on an understanding of good design or planning.

245

Polls taken during the second quarter of the twentieth century indicated that versions of the Colonial style (Fig. 19-1) were favored by the majority of homeowners. The houses, which they preferred and built, were constructed of brick, wood, and stone in the style of the Colonial homes of New England, of the middle colonies of New York, Pennsylvania, and New Jersey, and of the richer Georgian homes of the plantation owners in Virginia and Maryland. Those who turned to the past for their inspiration did not stop with the Colonial but drew upon the Early Republican style and upon the Greek and Roman revivals of both the North and the South. In fact, no single historical movement of the seventeenth, eighteenth, and early nineteenth centuries escaped being copied, adapted, and modified for the homes of all parts of the country. Pennsylvania homes of field stone were built throughout the Middle West, the cottage-like Dutch Colonial with its familiar dormers and white siding was popular in all parts of the country, while the Cape Cod house became symbolic of shelter for the modest-income group of almost every state in the union. Add to these the modern versions of the French and Spanish Colonial—their stucco walls and colorful tile roofs often out of place in the smoky atmosphere of our industrial cities—and our list of Eclectic homes of American derivation is substantially complete.

Rivaling the various phases of the Colonial for popularity were the many forms of English and French Gothic, especially the Tudor style, as in Fig. 19-2. The latter was used with much success in the larger homes of our cities and in the country homes on Long Island and in Westchester County, New York, and along the north shores of Boston and Chicago. In fact, few of our communities were overlooked in the construction of large homes of the wealthy copied rather directly from Compton Wynyates or of more modest homes of the middle-income group inspired by the charming stone cottages of the Cotswolds. Changing economic conditions, new ways of entertaining, and lack of domestic help have made Tudor Gothic manor houses somewhat out of date. Nevertheless, many homes were built in the characteristic style that employed crenelated balustrades, pointed-arch doorways, clustered chimneys with ornate brick details, and half timber combined with brick walls in the familiar diaper pattern. The interiors of many of these houses might have come

FIG. 19-3. Italian type house with low roof and stucco walls.

FIG. 19-4. Columns with round arches recall Renaissance style.

directly from Haddon Hall or Hampton Court Palace or from any of the smaller manor houses of the fifteenth century. The rooms had paneled walls, groups of casement windows in the form of bays, open-timber roofs or plastered ceilings with geometrical patterns; often they were filled with copies of Tudor and Elizabethan furniture to harmonize with the atmosphere of this medieval setting.

French domestic architecture was not without its influence on the homes of twentieth-century America. From the minor chateaux and farmhouse groups we borrowed the informal compositions of steep roofs, turrets, high chimneys, towers, tall French windows, areas of stucco and brick, and quoins—all familiar parts of the houses built a few decades ago. We also drew upon the architecture of sunny Italy for assistance in the design of many homes of the period. Here the arched loggia often formed the central motif of the entrance and gave an accent to the simple stucco walls with their regularly spaced and shuttered windows, Figs. 19-3 and 19-4. An Italian Renaissance cornice with brackets, together with a low-pitched tile roof of brilliant colors, usually completed the exterior composition.

Attempts on the part of the unskilled to copy the medieval Tudor Gothic of the more ambitious and well-designed homes resulted in a mongrel type of architecture which even the changes following World War II have not improved or modified. This was and is a kind of pseudomedieval architecture, a caricature of the buildings of rural England. Here false half timber, awkward roof arrangements ugly in appearance and wasteful of interior space, and the many materials of brick, stucco, and field stone were all combined in one small cottage to create an undesirable type of domestic shelter. In those communities where the blight of the false half-timber style did not strike, the less objectionable but nevertheless derivative Cape Cod cottage appeared in large numbers. In many suburban developments we find acres of these inoffensive but monotonously similar white houses, alike except for the brilliant colors of their roofs.

To the list of houses built during the first few decades of this century we must add one type that became typically American in its use and acceptance. This was the bungalow of the Middle West,

FIG. 19-5 (*opposite*). Residence in California, with a conspicuous Spanish ancestry, as shown in the stucco walls, tile roof, and richly decorated entrance with twisted columns. (*Photo by Hiller & Mott.*)

which has been copied in all parts of the country. It may have had its beginnings in the chalets of Switzerland since it used the same overhanging roof supported by large brackets and the same picturesque arrangement of shingles, siding, and rough stone work. It was usually a story or a story and a half high, with a deep porch or veranda across the front, composed of short, square wooden columns or posts set on a solid balustrade of shingles or stone, Fig. 19-6. The exterior walls were generally stained brown or green and trimmed with white. Perhaps its popularity may be attributed to its protection against the hot summers of the Middle West since its porch and overhanging roof served the same purpose as did the deep, two-story porticoes of the ante-bellum homes of the South.

In general, the homes worthy of our consideration were designed by reputable architects who combined good taste with a knowledge of function and materials. If these houses were clothed in the dress of European styles or American derivations, it was because of the lack of other forms of expression acceptable to the people of an expanding industrial culture who still turned to the past with confidence and to the future with uncertainty. These Eclectic homes were adequate as shelter; they have been satisfactory until the present, when changing economic conditions and ways of living have rendered them somewhat out of date.

These homes of the Eclectic movement, including those that are pleasing or ugly in appearance, have been built singly, one by one, as each individual owner found a desirable site, or in groups of several dozen or a hundred, sponsored and financed by public and private capital. To some of these have been applied the latest techniques in site planning, resulting in winding streets instead of the monotonous gridiron pattern of earlier subdivisions and providing ample open areas for light and air. In others, constructed without the services of qualified architects or site planners, are to be found most of the inferior homes of this country. The lots upon which these houses are built are too narrow; privacy, light, are unimportant.

INTERIORS

The plan of the typical twentieth-century "Colonial" house is familiar to most Americans. There are countless homes with a center

Fig. 19-6. A typical bungalow with projecting roof and large dormer, deep porch with short square posts set on piers, grouped windows, and dark upper siding. Early twentieth century.

Fig. 19-7. For the past few decades these small houses have appeared by the hundreds in new subdivisions across the land. Here are to be found many of the elements of a pseudomedieval style—half-timber decorations, stone buttresses, and stucco panels.

hall and stairway, on one side of which is the living room and, on the other, the dining room and kitchen. In the larger and more ambitious houses, there are many variations of this arrangement produced by the addition of other rooms. This Colonial-type house needs no further description.

The informal house of English or medieval derivation does not show the same degree of standardization typical of the smaller Colonial home; nevertheless there is a certain pattern distinguishable upon careful study. The entrance is still the center of interest and circulation; but the living room, dining room, and other units are arranged about this focal point in a variety of related schemes. Sometimes the living room is a few steps lower than the hall and has a high ceiling following the pitch of the roof, with exposed and decorative rafters and beams. In most of the English and Colonial houses, the two or three bedrooms, together with the bathroom, are located on the second floor.

In many of the small one-story cottages of the pseudo-English, "ranch house," and imitation Colonial types which crowd our suburban developments, the plans fall into two or three standardized patterns. The living room faces a busy street instead of a private garden —an example of poor orientation. The interior is likely to be ugly in composition and color, and the wall spaces and openings are arranged with little regard for the proper location of furniture or for direct circulation. These houses provide shelter for the physical, if not the spiritual, needs of the modest-income group; unfortunately they contribute little to the progress of house design in America.

The furniture and furnishings that filled the eclectic houses of the first half of the twentieth century were usually as heterogeneous as were the houses of the period. Stylistic furniture, both good and bad in design and use of materials, was turned out in unlimited quantities by countless factories all over the country. This was truly the age of "Grand Rapids" furniture. Our taste was catholic; we favored the Sheraton, Chippendale, Hepplewhite, and Queen Anne. We filled our houses with reproductions of Jacobean, Italian Renaissance, and a Monterey version of the Spanish; we borrowed from the Empire style popularized by Napoleon Bonaparte in the previous century.

20

THE RECENT DECADES

NEW PATTERNS OF LIVING

THE contemporary movement in architecture is not entirely the product of the present generation. While nontraditional architecture has become conspicuous only since the beginning of the second quarter of this century, its roots extend many decades into the nineteenth century. Significant changes paved the way for this new style. The inventions of the Industrial Revolution—the development of iron, steel, and reinforced concrete and the improvements in heating, illumination, and sanitation, both in Europe and America—have given to each succeeding generation a new hope for release from the inconveniences of our working and living activities. The growth of the modern movement in architecture, which has produced our skyscrapers, factories, and public buildings, is beyond the scope of this discussion; but it must be pointed out that the nontraditional house springs from the same social and economic forces that have built industrial America. It is true that the efficient modern home has lagged behind other architectural developments but now the growth of its popularity is gaining momentum. Once understood, nothing can stop its wide acceptance.

Regardless of our subject—whether it may be politics, economics, or architecture—the past is historical, the present is transitional, and the future is conjectural. Until the present moment in this discussion we have been dealing with history: reviewing in a chronological manner the growth of the homes of America as they have expressed the lives of past generations. We shall now look at the new architecture which, according to many, symbolizes present-day culture; and, by implication, we shall project the trend for future developments.

The present social and economic upheaval has been brought on by wars and depressions, by the shifting of buying and bargaining power, and by greater class consciousness and self-determination. Today there is not the exploitation of the masses that existed during the early days of the Industrial Revolution. Instead, the old balance of power has been delicately readjusted along new lines, and new forces are at work in all phases of our cultural pattern. These changes are reflected in the new forms of expression in music, painting, sculpture, literature, advertising, and architecture. Nothing escapes change; the home and family life are different because of new attitudes and practices.

Modern house planning and design have been swept along irresistibly by the acceptance of modern industrial and commercial architecture. Efficient home planning is borrowed from scientifically conceived workplaces. Industry develops a direct pattern for the routing of materials through the factory; the husband and housewife realize that wasteful extravagance in traditional design and uneconomical use of space may be eliminated in the home by the same careful study of paths of circulation. During the past one hundred years, significant changes have taken place in the manufacture of capital and consumer goods. Industry has changed from hand work to mass production and the lives of people in all social and economic strata have been profoundly affected. All except the most indigent have many of the appliances for convenient, if not comfortable, living; they benefit by the development of vehicles for rapid and pleasant transportation. Homes are no longer restricted to the smoky environs of the factory but may be built in the rural atmosphere of the suburbs. The modern factory and office have led the way in the design of light and comfortable furniture and the home has benefited by these improvements.

The tempo of life has increased and the modern house is rapidly becoming geared to this new pace. In spite of many material blessings, present-day existence is much more complex than in our grandmother's day. While many of our tasks are performed for us, we are constantly harassed by appointments and demands, by regulations and laws, by taxes and fees. Our homes should be as simple and efficient as possible to serve as a relief from the worries of our industrial world. It is possible that, while the housewife of a few generations ago may have worked harder in a physical sense, the homemaker of today often has a more harried existence. In the old days, the mother busied herself with the fundamental activities related to cooking, cleaning, and caring for the children. Nothing more was expected of her; generally, home was a workplace. Today she must be a social partner for her husband, help promote civic ventures, and carry on cultural and educational activities for her own development. In order to do all these things, she must have the assistance of outside agencies which fortunately have come to her rescue. Much of her family's food is prepared for her, much of her cleaning is done by commercial organizations. Other functions formerly performed in the home are now more efficiently cared for by other means and, as a result, the modern house has been developed into a new pattern to fit the needs of the twentieth-century family.

MECHANIZATION

Many of the improvements in twentieth-century family life and homes have been made possible by the increased mechanization of contemporary society. In fact, the history of the physical aspects of family life may be written in terms of the equipment of the cave, hut, cabin, or house. However, mechanization is not restricted to devices that are moved by or function with the aid of scientific forces. Mechanization results when any mechanical aid or tool is made and used to increase the power and efficiency of human hands and when human hands create useful equipment for better living. When we realize that the stool, bench, and chair, together with the table, chest, and bed, are instruments that help to place man above animal and that they have been, in general, part of all historical civilizations, we then recognize the encompassing significance of mechanization.

The influence of the modern machine began with the simple tools and implements of the pioneer. His saws and chisels, his plows and millstones—in fact, all the things with which he worked—were improved by use and by advances in technology. His stagecoach became a train and his raft a steamboat. And now the stagecoach, the train, the automobile, and the ship have all been outdistanced in time and space by the airplane and the rocket ship. The eighteenth-century shop with hand or water power has developed into the modern factory which now produces the equipment for the further mechanization of the contemporary home.

When we look closely at past and present domestic devices that have aided people in cooking, eating, reclining, and sleeping and at those with which people have secured protection and comfort, we may see how mechanical things reflect the culture of each period. We also realize how equipment, either that which works or that which serves, distinguishes one architecture from another. The present-day Eclectic house differs little from the eighteenth-century Colonial house except for the mechanical equipment. When a city dweller buys an old house in the country, a high degree of comfort and good living may be had merely by the installation of central heating, running water, and electrical current.

The kitchen has probably shown the most uninterrupted and consistent mechanization of any part of the house. This area has undergone many changes from the days of the early colonists through the nineteenth century to the present. Thus the kitchen has increased in efficiency, if not, nostalgically, in the matter of romantic appeal. The fireplace, with its backbreaking crane and kettles, gave way to the wood- or coal-burning kitchen stove with its ashes and smoke; the stove was then replaced by the gas and electric range, as seen in Fig. 20-3. The hand pump has been supplanted by the sink with running hot and cold water. The automatic dishwashing machine has taken the place of manual labor on the part of the housewife. The icehouse and the iced refrigerator have given way to the modern electric refrigerator and the freezing compartment. The home laundry has moved from the tub on the back porch or yard to the basement and finally to the modern first-floor utility room with its devices for the complete washing, drying, and ironing of clothing and linen.

The transformation of the bathroom into a comfortable and efficient unit of the house is a familiar chapter in the history of mechanization. The modern bathroom, with its provisions for personal sanitation, is a far cry from the scene of the old-time Saturday night bath in the tub on the kitchen floor or of the morning's ablutions with the pitcher and bowl on the commode in the bedroom. The fireplace as a heating unit was replaced by the cast-iron stove; the stove gave way to the various forms of central heat supplied by warm air, steam, hot water, and electric coil, all directed to the various rooms of the house and to every section of each room. Elsewhere in the house, mechanization has taken over; work activities are made

FIG. 20-1. Early American kitchen. Stephen Daniel house, Salem, Mass.

FIG. 20-2. Inefficient, ugly, and unromantic nineteenth-century kitchen.

FIG. 20-3. Efficient mechanized kitchen of the twentieth century.

easier and life is more comfortable. Cleaning is no longer a matter of raising dust with a broom but, instead, is a sanitary attack upon dirt with a vacuum cleaner and its various attachments. Even as this is written, new equipment for making housework easier is being designed and manufactured. It will be on the market tomorrow to provide an even greater degree of comfort in the home.

The history of mankind and of his dwellings could also be written in terms of artificial light. For thousands of years darkness was a foe to the progress of man, even though it might have been a friend to sleep and a cover from enemies. For centuries darkness yielded only slowly to the conquest by man-made light. In the early days of the colonies, man's working day was from sunup to sundown; the winter evenings in the home were short and generally unproductive of thought and action. The modern home with its efficient illumination has raised man to his highest level of intellectual and spiritual attainment by making him independent of the sun for light. Each generation has secured a greater degree of comfort through the development of better methods of illumination. Candles, oil lamps, and gas lights were the best that the earlier periods could produce but they are archaic in terms of present-day light sources scientifically designed for visual comfort.

Improvements for comfortable living have not been confined to methods of heating, cooking, cleaning, and illumination. The furniture and equipment of the modern house have been made more comfortable than any of earlier days. Contemporary designers have made a science out of furniture construction and, apparently for the first sustained period in American history, have created furniture that is directly related to human anatomy. Furniture design is no longer a matter of following the forms created by architecture but is, instead, concerned with a scientific approach to the correct proportions of chairs, tables, and storage cabinets for comfortable use. In addition, more attention is now given to the grouping of furniture for conversation and vision instead of for formal balance and effect, as was once the case. The stiff, uncompromising parlor of the nineteenth century, with its ugly and uncomfortable horsehair-covered sofas and chairs, has been transformed into a livable and comfortable area for games, conversation, and music.

The foregoing paragraphs focus attention on the fact that mechanization, together with improvements in construction, planning, and design, has increased the comforts of the modern family—all in response to a basic need. It may truthfully be said that much of the material progress in the world and most of the growth of a higher type of family life and shelter have been largely due to the desire of people for easier and more economical ways of performing work activities and for greater protection, safety, and comfort in domestic activities. It may also be said that much of the improvement in the techniques of living has been made because man is fundamentally lazy. He is always seeking an easier and, in progressive nations, a better way of carrying on his daily activities. Dull and backward people are content, year after year, to continue their backbreaking work with crude utensils and tools and to endure the discomfort of inadequate shelter and furnishings. But not so with those of progressive nations. Stupid laziness retards the development of efficient homes; intelligent laziness encourages domestic architecture of the highest order. The homes of America have improved in comfort because the people of America have been inquisitive and ingenious as they have sought a more pleasant existence.

ATTITUDES

While the nontraditional house is rapidly gaining favor, in some quarters the sentimental attitude toward the home is still almost as strong as it was during the Gothic Revival period of the last century. The romance of the rose-covered gate, the picket fence, and the dormer window still persists in spite of the acceptance of the blessings of science so conspicuous in other types of buildings. This is partly due to the preference of many people for regimentation. Conformation to an established social practice gives a feeling of security—a security that may not be physical in its application but one that is psychological in its appeal. It is easy to follow the line of least resistance and to build according to established traditions. However, today many people have both the courage and the desire to break with the past in the matter of house planning and to enjoy the benefits of science together with the beauties of contemporary design and materials. It is the homes of these fortunate people that we illustrate on the accompanying pages.

Not only are houses different in appearance from those built by former generations but they are also different by the place which they occupy in the lives of people. A house is no longer built deliberately as the family homestead to be passed down from eldest son to eldest son. People are less static than they were decades ago. Class distinctions are less pronounced and permanent; new opportunities are presented to each new generation. Young America is on the move; it does not want to be tied to big houses and many belongings. This change may be viewed with mixed emotions; perhaps this mobility is not a complete blessing. The man who once worked on the land tilled by his ancestors now often wanders from job to job. Home becomes an apartment with modern labor-saving devices but with few of the ties that once bound the family circle.

Perhaps it is to be regretted that the dignified old Colonial house, constructed so substantially and with such loving care, has lost its appeal and that the children and grandchildren do not care to live there any longer, adding their pleasures and sorrows to the memories which still cling to the walls. But architecture cannot force an issue, it cannot create a social pattern; architecture merely reflects the lives of people. Today family ties have been broken, children now scatter to new opportunities in distant cities; the size of the family has decreased and large homes are no longer necessary or desirable. The new architecture beckons and today houses are built, not for future generations, but for present needs. They are designed for maximum convenience and comfort; and, instead of serving as show places to impress friends, they are built or purchased with the same frugal care that one exercises in buying an automobile or a suit of clothes. The homes of earlier generations had drawing rooms and grand staircases; the homes of today are simply enclosed space with arrangements kept flexible for adaptation to changes in family life.

Modern houses are, in general, much smaller than the mansions of the Georgian period, the ante-bellum days, the Industrial Revolution, or the Eclectic homes of a generation ago. We have seen the number of servants diminish until the large house is both a physical and psychological burden. Entertaining in the home is now usually confined to small, intimate parties—the hotels and clubs have taken over the grand affairs of a few decades ago. Recreation is to be found elsewhere than in the home, as commercial agencies provide every conceivable type of amusement. The influence of television on family life and family recreation is still problematical; it may be revolutionary in its impact on domestic activities and shelter.

Chapter 21

RELEASE FROM TRADITION

THE PIONEERS

DURING the early part of the twentieth century America was generally so engrossed in building Renaissance monuments that it missed the significance of the work of those pioneers in Europe who were creating new forms to shelter the activities of man. But to those who had their finger on the architectural pulse of that continent, the names of Josef Hoffmann, Peter Behrens, Auguste Perret, and others were meaningful. These men gave new and strange shapes to the schools, factories, and houses that came from their fertile brains by way of their facile pencils. French architects, with Perret as their leader, perfected the use of reinforced concrete. This new material demanded its own type of exterior treatment and encouraged flexibility in planning and freedom from structural limitation.

In addition to the influences of new materials and types of construction, there was a revolt in all the arts. The realism and the sentimentality of the then current style of painting were discarded for cubism and its related movements, in which the artist eliminated the superficialities of subject matter and reduced forms to planes and surfaces. The architect borrowed the spirit and angularity of cubism and found in the simplicity of the new architecture a willing recipient of its geometrical forms.

By the end of the first quarter of the twentieth century the new winds of the modern movement were beginning to blow with noticeable vigor. The house was becoming "a machine for living in," according to the pronouncements of Le Corbusier; and architecture, in general, with its emphasis on the mechanical, was efficient and

261

impersonal. Europe was again leading the way with such architects as Walter Gropius, Mies van der Rohe, and J. J. P. Oud. The International style made its appearance and created a furore about whether it was international in its scope or consistent enough to be a style. This style was based on the importance of functionalism as a mechanical device and the relative unimportance of appearance as a humanizing influence. It seemed to be symbolized by a boxlike architecture, composed of white stucco walls, combined with large expanses of glass, flat roofs which often served as terraces, and lally, or iron, columns supporting corners of projecting second-story units. It was an important phase in the development of the contemporary house in that it broke so completely with the restraints of traditional architecture. It cleared the air for a scientific approach to the planning of homes and, after the first fanatical espousal of stark simplicity was humanized, went ahead to lead the way in the development of other related forms of expression.

In spite of the international character of the movement, the style, once having achieved a divorce from the past, continued in a normal development to acquire definite nationalistic characteristics. As each country embraced the style, the influences of climate, customs, and indigenous materials began to modify and soften the mechanical qualities of the basic design. A number of architects who had led in this movement and who had made a name for themselves in their own countries, came to America for the richer opportunities that this country offers. Among these were Walter Gropius, whose own home is shown in Fig. 21-5, Marcel Breuer, Mies van der Rohe, and Eliel Saarinen. With their splendid sense of fitness and fine regard for appearance, they have been, for several decades, leaders in the design of structures of all types. These men have joined the many equally renowned architects of American birth and training and together they are leading the world in the creation of efficient and beautiful architecture.

Even before some of the leaders in Europe were experimenting with new materials and forms, Frank Lloyd Wright, pupil of Louis Sullivan, had opened his office in Chicago in 1893 for the practice of architecture. In the early 1900's he began to build in the Windy City and its environs a new type of house which was to secure for him more fame in foreign countries than in America. These houses—

FIG. 21-1. Coonley house, Riverside, Illinois. Early house by Frank Lloyd Wright, 1908. The horizontal lines of the structure, low roof with deep projections, and rows of windows above balconylike flower boxes reflect the individuality of the designer.

continued since with only minor modifications in materials and treatment—were low horizontal masses with overhanging roofs, houses which seemed to repeat the lines of the prairies of which they were a part. The Coonley house, Riverside, Illinois, Fig. 21-1, built in 1908, exemplifies these characteristics. Here was a brick and stone architecture combined with wood for interior treatment as well as for exterior structure.

Wright believed that the house should repeat the qualities of nature. He saw the house, not as a cave, confining and stifling, but simply as a roof above an openness below, revealing pleasant vistas of hills and valleys. He saw man living in space but not cut off from it. Thus a sense of freedom which comes from a close association with nature was the keynote of the architecture of Frank Lloyd Wright, a freedom which has been retained in the best work of the architects of the present decade. One of his recent houses, built at Bloomfield Hills, Michigan, Fig. 21-2, illustrates many of these qualities.

FIG. 21-2. House at Bloomfield Hills, Michigan. Frank Lloyd Wright, architect. View looking toward car port and rear of house. The rectangular brick wall surfaces and the projecting balcony opening from the living area are typical of the work of Mr. Wright. (*Photo by Joe Munroe.*)

FIG. 21-3. Interior of above house, view from entrance hall looking past fireplace into living room. Note use of brick and simple wood surfaces on the interior. (*Photo by Joe Munroe.*)

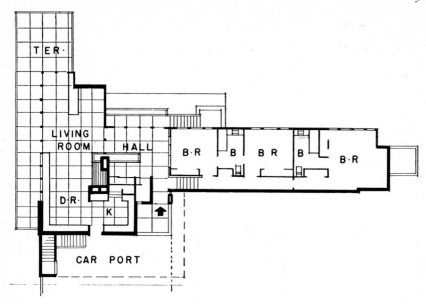

Fig. 21-4. Plan of house, opposite, by Frank Lloyd Wright. Pronounced separation of living quarters from sleeping area. Open quality throughout living space.

THE SPACE HOUSE

The modern houses of today, as distinguished from those based on period architecture, make use of the inventions and products of modern science. But the "machine for living in" as developed by the early Internationalists has had much of its starkness, coldness, and crudeness eliminated through a greater regard for appearance. Man does not walk around with his bones showing; he was very sensibly conceived with his structural system and mechanical equipment concealed and his angular contours softened. And so with the best of modern architecture. The early expressions were essentially engineering feats; the later ones are a happy compromise between function and appearance. The structure and equipment are no longer entirely exposed; they are expressed, yet concealed. Beauty has assumed its proper importance along with construction and materials.

It is becoming increasingly difficult to write emphatically and finally, if one ever could, about contemporary architecture. The

Fig. 21-5. Home of Walter Gropius, architect, Lincoln, Mass. View of rear from garden, showing living room and enclosed porch. Plain rectilinear masses and surfaces, combined with ribbon windows, are characteristic of this phase of the contemporary.

Fig. 21-6. Interior of above house, looking from dining area into living room. Flexible use of space. Compare simplicity of decoration with richness of Georgian examples, Figs. 4-16 and 8-10.

FIG. 21-7. Principal elevation of Gropius house, showing shelter for entrance and spiral stairway to second-floor terrace. Note angularity of various exterior elements.

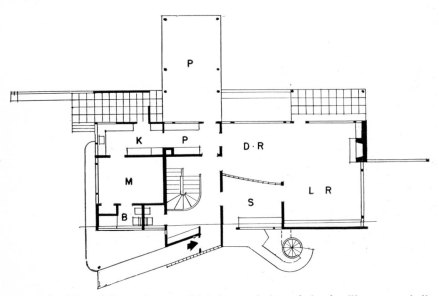

FIG. 21-8. Plan of above house, which is a variation of the familiar center-hall arrangement. The major living spaces face the privacy of the garden at the rear.

modern movement is in such a state of flux that any analysis of its characteristics may be out of date before the ink is dry on the page. A few years ago the modern house seemed to be reduced to a definite pattern. It had a flat roof supported by walls of brick or tile, usually covered with white stucco. Unsymmetrical massing was as characteristic of the style as was the symmetrical facade of the Colonial period, while corner windows were as typical as were the regularly spaced windows of the earlier homes.

But just as we were complacently settled with this type of modernism, a later and more informal treatment appeared. Perhaps it originated in California where the mild climate encourages informal living and open planning, as in Fig. 21-9. In these more recent homes, which have appeared in all parts of the country as the influence of climate has been defeated somewhat by the ingenuity of science, we have the ultimate thus far in the development of fluid space; there is little or no barrier between enclosed volume and the great outdoors. These houses of California and their reflections elsewhere in regions of comparable climate illustrate the influence of weather, materials, and modes of living on domestic architecture. Such houses, often built of wood, as in Fig. 21-14, are simple and unpretentious and permit a comfortable existence inside and out, with a minimum amount of equipment and care.

Here we have houses built by talented architects in a way that must be a joy to one who is sensitive to the harmonious coordination of function, materials, and beauty of line, texture, and color. The exteriors defy any standardized description. They are usually one story in height, or two if on a sloping site; they are low and horizontal in direction; they combine wood, stone, and brick in ways that lack the pretentiousness of earlier days; their roofs are flat or low pitched in contrast to the high roofs of the Colonial and English periods.

PLANNING

The development of the plan of the American house is a history of American life and progress. The early hut, thrown together in haste by the Pilgrims as protection against the weather or by the pioneer on his way across the plains, probably had only one room.

In it were carried on all of the activities connected with family life. There was little or no privacy; all members of the family joined in the group activity of eating, conversing, and sleeping. There was little freedom of effort within the house; the individual was subordinate to the group.

The plan of the Early American house of the seventeenth century called for two or more rooms, except in the earliest examples. This increase in size permitted some separation of household activities but still did not afford the privacy that was to come later in the development of the American home. Many of the living activities were still centered in the major room, and group participation was more conspicuous than individual freedom. In these homes and those that followed the frontier, the privacy of bedrooms was sacrificed for simplicity of circulation. Hallways had not yet become an important part of domestic architecture.

During the eighteenth and nineteenth centuries there were gradual improvements in planning and in the assignment of special functions to the various rooms of the house, as in the typical New England Colonial house, shown in Fig. 21-13B. This specialization in the use of rooms increased in the Victorian period, Fig. 21-13C and reached its climax during the Gilded Age when, in the homes of the wealthy, there was a multiplication of units to meet every conceivable requirement. There were large kitchens, butler's pantries, formal dining rooms, parlors, drawing rooms, and libraries. There were ball rooms for social events and conservatories for the growing of the flowers for these festive occasions. This was truly the age of complexity in planning.

Today the trend is toward simplification. The one-room efficiency apartment is an example of this desire for a minimum type of shelter. Here a bed may be pulled out from the wall, a closet may contain the kitchen equipment, and a small cubicle may hold the bathroom facilities. In the contemporary nontraditional house there is a tendency to combine the cooking, dining, and living requirements in one large area or at least into one that does not have the definite barriers typical of earlier homes. Because of changing economic conditions, the lack of domestic help, and new attitudes toward family life, we are returning to a simpler type of domestic architecture. We have borrowed the simplicity of the primitive hut but we have tempered

FIG. 21-9. House in Los Angeles, California. Richard J. Neutra, architect. Exterior view, showing informality of composition combining vertical and horizontal lines and surfaces. Interesting contrast of direction, color, and texture in the use of materials. *(Photo by Julius Shulman.)*

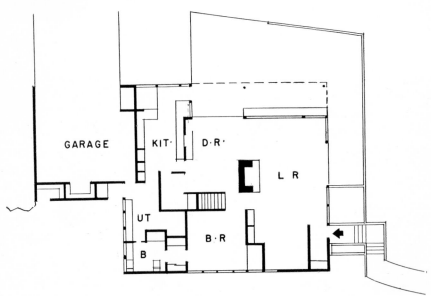

FIG. 21-10. Plan of above house, illustrating how open and flexible arrangements are possible with the combined living and dining area. Terraces continue living space.

Fig. 21-11. View of indoor and outdoor living area in house by Richard J. Neutra. Here is interpenetration or uninterrupted flow of space, with almost complete lack of sense of definite enclosure or of rigid separation of rooms as in traditional houses. *(Photo by Julius Shulman.)*

Fig. 21-12. Living room in above house, combining livability, simplicity, and spaciousness. Interesting contrasting textures and dramatic play of light and shade. *(Photo by Julius Shulman.)*

this crude simplicity with the comforts afforded by modern equipment. Ours is a planned and deliberate simplicity instead of the meagerness of the backwoodsman who was ignorant of or lacked the tools for convenient living.

As is always the case with good architecture, the modern movement begins with sound planning. However, it is planning in which the arrangement is no longer determined by a Colonial, Greek, or Tudor facade. It is planning for human needs in terms of the modern family. Changing concepts of leisure, of household tasks, and essential equipment combine to produce a plan pattern that is quite unlike any of earlier days. It lacks standardization, it cannot be reduced to a formula. Gone is the symmetrical plan with the center hall, and instead there is the informal plan which fits the site, provides proper orientation for sun and wind, and expresses the individual and collective needs of all members of the family.

The typical plan of today, if one exists, is usually an open arrangement that allows the major living units to flow into each other with a minimum amount of interference, as indicated in the plan in Fig. 21-10. The combined living and dining area is reduced to its essentials and its simple furniture reflects the multi-purpose use of the area. Usually this living space faces toward the privacy of the garden or lawn at the rear; the friendly days, when the front porch was the gallery from which the doings of the villagers were observed, vanished when the slow tempo of the nineteenth century gradually changed to the ever quickening pace of the twentieth century.

The definitely segregated cubicles or rooms created by permanent walls are now suggested rather than defined. Built-in furniture, screens, and curtains are now used to create the illusion of separation. This relationship between furnishings and architecture is one of the most conspicuous characteristics of the new movement (Fig. 21-3). As we look back over our survey of the homes of America, we realize that, until the contemporary period, the house and its furniture were two separate and distinct things. The house was merely the architectural shell; it was built according to the traditions of the current style, and the furniture and furnishings were added or changed by each succeeding family. Too often there was little relationship between the architecture and the furniture. The walls and windows were not designed for the chairs, sofas, tables, and beds that were

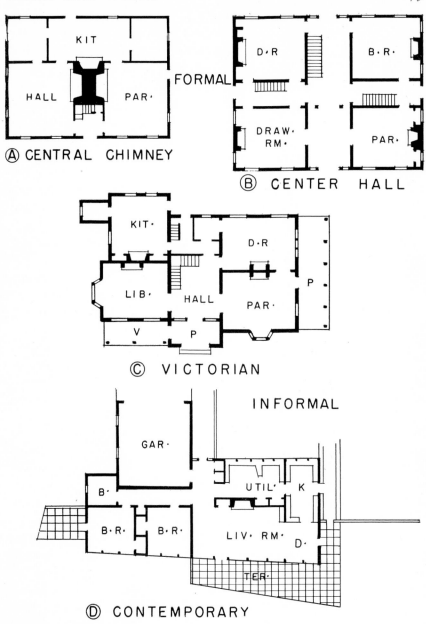

Fig. 21-13. Plan development through the various important periods, from the compact Early American type to the informal, open, and rambling contemporary treatment.

Fig. 21-14. House near Stockton, California. Wurster, Bernardi and Emmons, architects. A simple, pleasing horizontal house with redwood siding. A direct and unpretentious type of treatment which has been copied with varying degrees of success in many parts of the country. (*Photo by Roger Sturtevant.*)

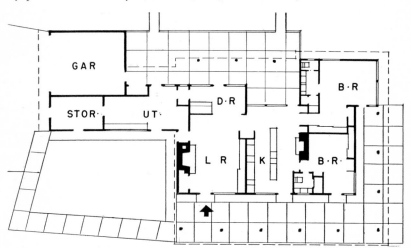

Fig. 21-15. Plan of above house. Living room, dining space, and kitchen combined into one integrated living area. The covered terraces are conspicuous features.

Fig. 21-16 (*opposite*). Interior view, showing clear-story lighting. (*Photo by Roger Sturtevant.*)

Fig. 21-17. House in St. Louis, Missouri. Harris Armstrong, architect. A country place in the contemporary manner, as expressive of present-day culture as Westover, Fig. 8-8, was of eighteenth-century life. *(Photo by Tom Leonard.)*

to occupy the room. Now much of the furniture is either built in or at least designed as a part of the interior. The activities that normally belong to the room are studied in terms of the necessary equipment; designing of comfortable and efficient furniture for each family activity makes proper provision for conversation, reading, music, and games.

The illusion and actual presence of spaciousness, created by the elimination of solid walls, is encouraged by the use of large areas of glass to give an uninterrupted view, admit the winter sun, eliminate glare from isolated openings, and, psychologically, promote the feeling of the interpenetration of man-made and natural space. This is well illustrated in the house in Fig. 21-12. This arrangement permits the use of concentrated wall surfaces as backgrounds for decorative effects and functional equipment. The walls and ceilings are without any suggestion of the moldings, pilasters, and panels characteristic of traditional architecture. These surfaces are usually plain; the only interest obtained is by the contrasting textures and colors of the

Fig. 21-18. Interior of living room of house shown on opposite page. Here new and simple forms, surfaces, and textures are blended into an informal and pleasing composition typical of the best of the modern homes. *(Photo by Tom Leonard.)*

stone, brick, plywood, glass, plaster, and other materials used as surface treatment.

The furniture and furnishings accompanying the modern movement in architecture are so varied in character that they defy brief description. Again the spirit is based on functionalism; European and American designers have produced many versions of functional furniture to fit the anatomy and the activities of men, women, and children. Plywood forms have been molded into shapes calculated to conform to all positions of the human body, while tubular metal has been combined with fabrics to produce a variety of pieces of everyday equipment, as in Figs. 21-11 and 21-18. Upholstered chairs and sofas are low, wide, deep, and comfortable; they are informal and quite in contrast with the formal, high, stiff, and uncomfortable pieces of stylistic furniture. The desks, tables, chests, and other similar objects again follow no definite pattern but are made in a variety of shapes to fit the space and the purpose for which they are designed. Free and irregular geometrical shapes in the form of trapezoids and parallelograms are often used instead of the more regular and orthodox areas. Fine woods and interesting finishes replace moldings for decorative effects. Modern printed and woven fabrics, usually with abstract designs, are used conspicuously as drapery and upholstering materials.

The modern movement in architecture is no superficial veneer applied to old structural forms; in fact, the entire style can attribute its birth, growth, and acceptance to the development of new methods of construction and new materials for the building industry. The structural systems of the modern house differ radically from those of earlier types of architecture. Formerly all walls were bearing walls; they carried a load and supported a floor or a roof. The non-traditional space house has been developed with the aid of modern engineering which has released architecture from the restrictions of earlier days. Isolated points of support in the form of slender columns of iron or steel or piers of masonry, together with trusses and cantilevered slabs, make up the structural system of modern houses. Distances between walls are no longer regulated by the strength and length of floor joists; instead spaces may be of almost any reasonable size and shape and walls may be used merely as enclosures. Walls, thus, are no longer weight bearing but are simply skins of glass, metal, wood, or synthetics, as in Fig. 21-11. All this contributes to the lightness of modern domestic architecture and helps to give it that dynamic, soaring quality which distinguishes it from the static character of the traditional styles.

Prefabrication, while in its infancy, promises to solve many of the problems facing the homebuilder, especially those related to costs, speed of construction, and simplicity of design. Many interpretations of this method, as distinguished from the custom-made type where each operation is performed on the job, are being tried by modern builders. Each system of prefabrications has its own particular advantages, distinguished by the material used and the unit fabricated at the factory; however, it still remains for mass production to establish prefabrication as a dominant factor in the building industry. Prefabrication will grow in importance, as it has since the days when entire kitchen and bathroom units were first assembled in the factory and stairways and window and door frames and appurtenances were made ready for installation on the job. Prefabrication is an established fact but its influence on the plan and appearance of the modern house has not yet become entirely evident.

One of the most conspicuous characteristics of the modern house is the inclusion of controlled environment. For several decades modern man has been accustomed to spending much of his working time in an artificial climate but only recently has he given serious attention to living at home in a comfortable environment. By clinging to traditional ideas of coziness in the home, man has refused to take complete advantage of the instruments of science to condition his hours of relaxation. Too often in the past "design" has dominated our homes; now science has become a partner in the planning of our most intimate shelter areas.

The architect of the contemporary nontraditional house draws upon the science of electronics, chemistry, physics, hygiene, optics, statics, construction, and even psychology for his source of inspiration and knowledge. The modern house shelters the activities of contemporary family life, but it does so by supplying adequate sanitation, lighting, heating, and acoustical treatment. The thermometer is no longer sufficient in the control of thermal environment; humidity and air movement combine with temperature to produce physical comfort. The modern house—with radiant and solar heating, insulation, air conditioning, and double glazing, all of which are aided by other developments of engineering—has become a carefully disguised laboratory, catering to the wishes and comfort of all members of a family. New light sources and their scientific location within the house have opened new vistas in illumination and encouraged new approaches to interior design. Improvements in sanitation have kept pace with other branches of mechanical equipment and have provided bathrooms and laundries more efficient and pleasant than any that have gone before. Objectionable sounds have been engineered out of the house or isolated by absorptive and reflective surfaces. Music is confined to its proper area, sleeping rooms are insulated against unwanted intrusions. Thus the house is finally catching up with technological developments.

SYNTHESIS

As we pause to realize how often the word "modern" is used to describe the homes of today, we are impressed with the inadequacy of the term and the inaccuracy of its application. Currently and popularly it distinguishes nontraditional houses from those that exhibit Colonial, English, or other stylistic details. Actually the homes of each of the great historical periods have been modern in that they expressed the materials, construction, and social order of the time. The adobe houses of the Southwest, the Early American dwellings of the Pilgrims, and the plantation homes of the Deep South were as modern as the knowledge of their builders would permit.

It is not fair for the ultraprogressive to scorn everything that is old and to compare, superficially, the period homes of the past with the machinelike houses of today. Old Colonial houses, when occupied today, may not be as convenient and comfortable as those of the contemporary period but they were built by men who knew only transportation by stage coach, illumination by candles, and artificial warmth from the fireplace. They were the product of an earlier culture and in the past they should remain, with newer expressions developing in accord with modern practices. The dignity, charm, and beauty of the Colonial, Georgian, Federal, and Roman and Greek Revival periods—born of craftsmen who knew the properties of materials and who were willing to exploit them with loving care—will perhaps never again be duplicated. To lovers of the traditional, we can only say that the new architecture is trying to express the ever changing way of living; the new homes are nontraditional, just as modern refrigerators, comptometers, toasters, automobiles, airplanes, or fountain pens are unlike their counterparts of a generation ago.

Of one thing we can be certain; tomorrow's homes will be unlike those of today. They will develop, not by formula or the wishes of either an individual or groups of individuals, but according to an ever changing social, economic, and physical environment. Houses with solid walls will enclose and shelter, they will afford maximum privacy and shield the timid from the world. Houses with open walls will also shelter but they will embrace the outside, permitting the bold to live as an integral part of surrounding nature. The character of the homes of tomorrow rests in the hands of those who create them—the architects, builders, and homeowners. In turn, these individuals move, unpremeditatedly, in a society which is and will be in a state of constant change—their homes are bound to express the ever shifting trends. We have seen the Colonial, the Victorian, and the contemporary; we can only guess at the "modern" of succeeding generations.

INDEX

[Italic figures indicate illustrations.]

Abbot house, Andover, Mass., *1*
Adam, Robert, 159; house by, *156*
Anderson house, Ann Arbor, Mich., 200, *202*, 204
Armstrong, Harris, house by, *276*, 277
Atwood house, Chatham, Mass., 58, *60*
Austin house, Paris, Ill., *234*

Bacon's Castle, Surry County, Va., 122, *123*
Battersea, Dinwiddie County, Va., *182*
Baum house, Cincinnati, Ohio, *174*, 176
Beauregard house, Chalmette, La., *209*, 210
Belle Grove, Frederick County, Va., *183*
Blacklock house, Charleston, S. C., *170*, 173
Bolduc house, Ste. Genevieve, Mo., *11*
Brafferton Hall, Williamsburg, Va., *135*
Brattle house, Cambridge, Mass., 78, *82*, 83, 86, 90
Bremo, Fluvanna County, Va., *181*, 185
Brewton house, *see* Miles Brewton house
Brice house, Annapolis, Md., 136, *137*

Brown house, Providence, R. I., 168, *169*
Browne house, Flushing, N. Y., *101*
Bruin house, Kerhonkson, N. Y., *13*
Burnside Plantation (The Houmas), Ascension Parish, La., *209*, 210

California, 21, 144
Campbell house, Mt. Carmel vicinity, Ohio, *202*
Cape Cod houses, 57, 58, *59*, *60*
Capen house, Topsfield, Mass., 43, 48, *56*
Carson house, Taos, N. M., *147*
Chaffee house, Windsor, Conn., *12*
Charleston, S. C., 138, 173; houses in, *13*, *139*, *141*, *142*, *170*, *208*
chimneys, 42, 70, 126, 130, 133
Classical architecture, 5, 6
Classical Revival, 178
Clemence house, Manton, R. I., 38, *40*, *41*, 50
climate, influences of, 4, 18, 19, 20, 25
Colonial houses: New England, 31; middle colonies, 95; South Atlantic, 121; Spanish, 145; French, 150; Eclectic, *244*
Conser house, Jefferson, Ore., *191*
contemporary houses, 265
Cook-Oliver house, Salem, Mass., *160*, *161*, 164

Coonley house, Riverside, Ill., *263*
cornices, *74, 75, 76, 78,* 83

Daniel house, Salem, Mass., *54, 257*
doorways, *see* entrances
Doric details, 73, *74*
Dutch Colonial architecture, 96, *97-103*
Dutch people, 92, 95; Pennsylvania "Deutsch," 26, 93, 108
Dyckman house, New York, 96, 102, *103*

Early American houses, 37, *40-59*
early American settlers, 31, 122
Eclecticism: life of period, 241; houses, *244-251*
entrances: Early American, 50; New England Colonial, 76, *79;* Post-Colonial, *162, 163, 165, 170, 171, 173, 175, 176, 180, 181;* Greek Revival, *199,* 200, *213*
environment (*see also* social order), 4, 5
exteriors: Early American, *41, 44, 45,* 48; New England Colonial, *71,* 73, 77, 78, *80, 81, 82, 83, 84;* middle colonies, 96, *97-115;* South Atlantic colonies, *123-142;* Spanish, 146, *147;* French, *151,* 152; Post-Colonial, 165, *also 160-183;* Greek Revival, 196, 197, *199-213;* Gothic Revival, *229, 230, 232, 233, 234;* Eclectic, *244, 245, 246, 247, 249, 251;* contemporary, 268, *also 263-277*

Fairbanks house, Dedham, Mass., *46*
Fatio house, St. Augustine, Fla., *145*
Federal period, 155
fireplaces, *49, 51, 52, 53,* 89
Fisher-Whiting house, Dedham, Mass., 70, *80,* 89
Ford house, Morristown, N. J., 112, *113*
Fort Johnson, Amsterdam, N. Y., 112, *114*
French influence, 149, 179, 235; buildings of, 150
frontier homes, 192
furniture: Early American, 55, 57;

New England Colonial, 91; Dutch, 102; Spanish, 146; Victorian, 224; Eclectic, 252; contemporary, 277

Georgian style, 6, 52, 65, 88, 108, 123, 155
German influence (*see also* Dutch), 94, 105
Girod house, New Orleans, La., 150, *151*
Glebe Hall, Charles City, Va., *123*
Gorgas house, Tuscaloosa, Ala., *213*
Gothic architecture, 6
Gothic Revival, 225, 227, *229,* 230, *233, 234*
Greek architecture, 5
Greek revival, 186, 195, 198, *199-213*
Greystone house, Pevely, Mo., *229*
Gropius, Walter, house by, *266, 267*

Hasbrouck house, Newburgh, N. Y., *98*
Hasbrouck, Jean, house, New Paltz, N. Y., *100*
Heyward-Washington house, Charleston, S. C., *139,* 140
Home house, London, Eng., *156*
Homewood, Baltimore, Md., *175, 176*
Hooper house, Marblehead, Mass., 75, 77, 83, 87
Houmas, the, *see* Burnside Plantation
Hull Sherwood house, Fairfield, Conn., 76, 78, *79, 84*
Hurst house, Dover, Ohio, *203,* 204

Industrial Revolution, 14, 187, 215, 228, 241, 253
interiors: Early American, 50; New England Colonial, 86; middle colonies, 113; Spanish, 146; Post-Colonial, 158; Greek Revival, 200; Victorian, 221-224; Eclectic, 250; contemporary, 276
Ionic details, 74
Izard house, Charleston, S. C., 140, *141*

Jefferson, Thomas, 182
Johnson Hall, Johnstown, N. Y., 112, *115*

Kimball house, Ipswich, Mass., 42, 47, 49, 52, 54
King cabin, Chewelah, Wash., 15
kitchens, 22, 50, 257
Knight-Short house, Newbury, Mass., 24, 76, 79

Liberty Hall, Frankfort, Ky., 171, 173
log cabin, Swedish, 9
Longfellow house, Cambridge, Mass., 69, 70, 71, 78, 83, 85
Loring-Emmerton house, Salem, Mass., 162, 164, 165
Louvre, Paris, 236

Mabie house, Rotterdam Junction, N. Y., 99
McIntire, Samuel, 159; houses by, 160, 164
Magnolia Grove, Greensboro, Ala., 211
mantels, see fireplaces
Martin house, Norwalk, Ohio, 169, 173
mechanization, 225
Melrose, Natchez vicinity, Miss., 206
Michie Tavern, Charlottesville vicinity, Va., 177
Miles Brewton house, Charleston, S. C., 140, 142
Monroe house, South Shaftsbury, Vt., 78, 79, 84, 85
Monticello, Charlottesville vicinity, Va., 180, 184
Morse-Libby house, Portland, Me., 237, 239
Morton-Corbett house, Ipswich, Mass., 46
Mount Airy, Warsaw, Va., 20, 110, 126, 127, 128
Mount Pleasant, Philadelphia, Pa., 110, 111

needs of people, 27
Neutra, Richard J., houses by, 2, 23, 270, 271
New England, 31, 61, 64, 66, 72
New Orleans, 150
Nike Apteros temple, 196

Old Hall, Norfolk, England, 109

Paca house, Annapolis, Md., 136, 137
Palladian details, 74, 78, 112, 165, 174
Palladio, Andrea, 68
Paris Opera House, 236
Payne house, East Hampton, N. Y., 104, 105
Peirce-Perry house, Newbury, Mass., 166
Pelzer house, Charleston, S. C., 13
Penshurst Place, Kent, England, 226
Phillips house, Salem, Mass., 163, 164, 165
Pilgrims, 31, 34, 35, 63, 217
pioneer, the: 19th century, 192; contemporary movement, 261
plans: Early American, 39; New England Colonial, 68, 69, 72; middle colonies, 102; South Atlantic, 125, 126; Spanish, 146; Post-Colonial, 157, 158; Greek Revival, 205, 207; Gothic Revival, 232; Victorian, 224, 236, 273; Eclectic, 250; contemporary, 268, 269, 273
Poplar Hall, Williamsburg vicinity, Va., 123
population, 16, 17
Post-Colonial period, 52, 78, 153; houses of, 158
prefabrication, 278
Puritans, 31, 34, 35, 62, 63

Quakers, 94, 105

Raleigh Tavern, Williamsburg, Va., 63
recuperation, 30
Renaissance architecture, 5, 6
Richardson, H. H., 240
Romanesque architecture, 6, 240
roofs, 50, 58, 85, 96, 108, 110, 121, 130, 145, 152, 158, 198, 268
Roper house, Charleston, S. C., 208
Roper house, Williamsburg, Va., 134
Ropes Memorial, Salem, Mass., 71, 85
Rosalie, Natchez, Miss., 207
Rose Hill, Lexington, Ky., 172

Ruggles house, Columbia Falls, Me., 168

salt-box house, 39, 42, 47
Scotch house, Saugus, Mass., 12
settled areas, 16, 17
Shadows, the, New Iberia, La., 212, 214
Shank house, Lancaster, Pa., 107
Sherwood house, see Hull Sherwood
Shirley, Charles City County, Va., 20, 23, 126
Skinner house, Hertford vicinity, N. C., 177
social order or environment: Early American, 34; New England Colonial, 61; middle colonies, 93; South Atlantic, 118; Spanish, 144; French, 149; Post-Colonial, 155; Greek Revival, 186-195; Gothic Revival and Victorian, 215-230; Eclecticism, 241; contemporary, 253
South, the, 20, 193
Spanish Custom House, New Orleans, La., 151
Spanish influence, 143; houses, 146
Spanish Treasury, St. Augustine, Fla., 11
stairways: Early American, 52, 54; New England Colonial, 86, 87
Stearns house, Oldtown, Mass., 76, 79, 83
Steelman house, Pennsauken township, N. J., 106, 108
Stratford Hall, Westmoreland County, Va., 20, 130, 131, 132, 133
Sturtevant, Widow, house, Albany, N. Y., 95, 97

Taft house, Cincinnati, Ohio, 174, 176
Taos, Ranchos de, New Mexico, 148
Third Empire, the, 235

Toll house, Cumberland Road, Md., 190
Trevett house, Marblehead, Mass., 70, 76, 81, 88, 90
Tucker house, Williamsburg, Va., 135

Van Alstyne house, Canajoharie, N. Y., 97
Vanderbilt house, New York, 220
Vhay house, Santa Barbara, Calif., 146, 148
Victorian life, 219, 225
Victorian houses, 223
Vignola, Giacomo Barozzi da, 67, 68
Virginia, 117; houses of, 124

walls: Early American, 48; New England Colonial, 75; middle colonies, 102, 110; South Atlantic, 124; Spanish, 146; Post-Colonial, 158; Greek Revival, 198; contemporary, 262, 268, 276
Westover, Charles City County, Va., 129, 130
Whipple house, Ipswich, Mass., 42, 44, 48
Williamsburg, Va., houses in, 21, 63, 123, 134, 135
Wilson house, Ann Arbor, Mich., 198, 199, 201, 204
Wister's Big House, Germantown, Pa., 108, 109
Woodford, Philadelphia, Pa., 110, 111
work activities, 29
Wright, Frank Lloyd, houses by, 53, 263, 264, 265
Wurster, Bernardi and Emmons, house by, 274, 275
Wythe house, Williamsburg, Va., 20, 21